KRONOS-HILL

Route to Arcadia

STADION
(630,8 ft. long)

Treasure Houses

I II III IV V VI VII VIII IX X XI XII

Entrance to Stadion

Starting Place

Altar

Metroon

Bases of Zanes

West Embankment of Stadion

East Wall of Altis

South Embankment of Stadion

LARGE

Altar of Zeus

Proedria (?)

FESTAL

Echo Portico

SQUARE

Oinomaos (?)

Eretrian Bull

Altar

Trojan Heroes

Praxiteles

Nike

Hippo- dameion (?)

S.E. Building

Peristyle of Nero's House

Octagon

Wall

Telemachos Mummius Rom. Triumphal Arch

Buleu- terion

Mediaeval

Channel of the

ALPHEIOS

(now filled up with rubbish)

Geograph. Anst. v. Wagner & Debes, Leipzig

OLYMPIA

THE LANDMARK LIBRARY

Chapters in the History of Civilization

The Landmark Library is a record of the achievements of humankind
from the late Stone Age to the present day. Each volume in the series
is devoted to a crucial theme in the history of civilization, and offers
a concise and authoritative text accompanied by a generous
complement of images. Contributing authors to The Landmark
Library are chosen for their ability to combine
scholarship with a flair for communicating their
specialist knowledge to a wider,
non-specialist readership.

OLYMPIA

The Story of the Ancient Olympic Games

ROBIN WATERFIELD

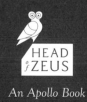

An Apollo Book

In memory of my time with
the Stragglers Running Club
and the Hayle Runners

This is an Apollo book, first published in the
UK in 2018 by Head of Zeus Ltd

Copyright © Robin Waterfield 2018

The moral right of Robin Waterfield to be
identified as the author of this work has been
asserted in accordance with the Copyright,
Designs and Patents Act of 1988.

1 3 5 7 9 10 8 6 4 2

A CIP catalogue record for this book is available
from the British Library.

ISBN (HB) 9781786691910
(E) 9781786691903

Designed by Isambard Thomas
Printed in Spain by Graficas Estella

Head of Zeus Ltd
First Floor East
5–8 Hardwick Street
London EC1R 4RG

WWW.HEADOFZEUS.COM

Prologue

As with many aspects of the ancient world, it is important to shed preconceptions before approaching the ancient Olympic games. Two stand out. First, the games were part of a religious festival, which is alien to our conception of an athletic meeting. Greek religion was largely a matter of practice rather than faith or belief, and athletic contests were viewed by everyone, contestants and spectators and judges, as participation in a religious rite. Perhaps the athletes felt that, in expending energy, they were offering it to the gods – to Zeus in particular, the presiding god of the Olympics. It is likely that they also considered the games entertainment for the gods; they were putting on a show in their honour.

Even the name Olympia had religious connotations, since it was derived from Mount Olympus, the highest mountain in Greece and the legendary home of Zeus and his extended family. Though he may not have been the original deity of the site, it was Zeus Olympius – Zeus of Olympus – to whom the games were dedicated. One of the first things the athletes did on arrival at Olympia was swear to Zeus that they would abide by the rules of the games. Fines for cheating and other infractions were paid to the god. Sacrifices to various gods and deities punctuated the festival and marked its climax. The Altis, the sacred precinct that constituted the heart of Olympia, was crammed with temples, altars and shrines to deities.

Second, since we are talking about 'sport', the word might trigger some inappropriate associations in the modern mind, in particular the notion of fair play and the idea that winning is less important than taking part.* The Greeks would have found this hard to understand; for them, winning was everything, and losers

---

* In the formulation of Baron Pierre de Coubertin, the man who devoted his life to reviving the ancient Olympics at the end of the nineteenth century: 'What is important in life is not success, but the struggle; what is essential is not winning, but competing well' (speech delivered on 24 July 1908).

felt ashamed of their failure. 'They cower in back alleys, avoiding their enemies, consumed by remorse at their failure,' said the poet Pindar of Boeotia.[1] That sentiment is of course not unknown in our day: 'Winning isn't everything,' said Vince Lombardi, the famous Green Bay Packers coach of the 1960s. 'It's the *only* thing.' In Greek terms, even though they sometimes noted second and third places as worthy attempts, it was only winning that showed you had earned the favour of the god.

George Orwell famously described sport (or international football matches, at any rate) as 'war minus the shooting'.[2] It is easy to think that the Olympic events were meant to foster skills useful in warfare; the ancient Greeks themselves used this argument to justify the enormous amounts of public money they spent putting on festivals involving athletic contests. It is a tempting idea – not least because the ancient Greek for athletic contest, *agōn*, was also a word for 'battle' – but not finally sustainable.

It is true that the case for a military origin for some of the events can easily be made – even for the foot races, if you think in terms of the distance a spear can be cast and followed up, and pursuit of a fleeing enemy; and for the long jump if you imagine it as practice for jumping ditches. But in fact skill at Olympic events would rarely translate into the kinds of abilities needed by a typical Greek soldier. Chariot racing, for example, first introduced in 680 BCE, remained an Olympic sport long after the Greeks had stopped using chariots in warfare. The seventh-century Spartan poet Tyrtaeus even doubted whether athletic ability necessarily developed the kind of courage needed in warfare. And in one of his plays Euripides, the fifth-century Athenian dramatist, had a character (we do not know who) say: 'Are they going to fight the enemy with discuses in their hands? Will they drive the foe from the fatherland by punching holes in their shields?'[3]

Euripides' sarcasm is justified. For fourteen successive Olympic festivals in the fifth century, starting with the 70th Olympiad in

500 BCE, there was a mule-cart race. This was clearly not meant to simulate anything that might happen in warfare. Moreover, there were no contests for team sports, which would presumably have been useful in a military context. For the Greeks, the games were an end in themselves; they were driven by love of competition, pride and patriotism, just as modern sportspeople are. The connection between war and sport worked only in the sense that both activities developed strength, endurance, discipline and courage, and because the ethos (and hence the vocabulary) of athletic competition mirrored that of warfare, both requiring violence restrained by respect for regulations.

overleaf
The Altis as an archaeological site. Note especially the temple of Zeus at the top, and the square Hotel Leonidas at the bottom left.

12   O L Y M P I A

Sacred Olympia

Best of all is water, and gold, bright as
*   firelight, gleams*
More than all other worldly wealth. But,
*   dear soul of mine,*
If you want a true contest to celebrate, just
*   as you need search*
The barren skies for no bright star more
*   warming than the sun,*
So the supreme games of which to sing are
*   those of Olympia.*

(Pindar, *Olympian Odes* 1.1–12)

So sang Pindar of Boeotia, the most famous of the praise-poets of the late sixth and early fifth centuries BCE. Winners of events at the major sporting festivals of ancient Greece commissioned poets such as Pindar to translate ephemeral victory into eternal fame. And they have, arguably, been as successful in that aim as they were in athletic competition, for Pindar's victory odes are still read today, nearly 2,500 years after his death and about 2,800 years after the running of the first Olympic race.

It was a meeting of A-list celebrities, in this case a monarch and a popular songwriter. This poem was commissioned by Hiero, famous throughout the Mediterranean world not just as the ruler of one of the greatest Greek cities, Sicilian Syracuse, but as the effective ruler of all the Greeks of Sicily and arguably the most powerful man in Europe at the time. He had won the horse race at the Olympic games of 476, and he chose to pay Pindar's steep fee so that the world, and especially his rivals, would know of his achievement. Nor was this the only time he got Pindar to celebrate his athletic victories.[1] Typically, Pindar would have not only written the words and music, but trained the chorus that sang the ode at its first public performance.

Olympia lies in the northwest of the Peloponnese, the great peninsula of southern Greece. Much of the centre of the Peloponnese is rugged and mountainous, but the mountains are surrounded by coastal plains, and Olympia is situated on one of these, in a beautiful river valley overlooked by the steep-sided Hill of Cronus. Two rivers meet at Olympia – the lesser Cladeus and the great Alpheus, one of the few rivers of southern Greece that has water all the year round. The site is low-lying and humid; bullfrogs and giant reeds abound, and in ancient times people prayed to Zeus, the Averter of Flies, pleading with him to keep the pests at bay. Believers insisted that it worked: the Roman writer Aelian, writing in the late second or early third century CE, reported that during the Olympic festival the flies took themselves over to the other side of the Alpheus, away from the proceedings.[2]

Although at first the Olympic festival was attended largely by local contestants, it was well placed to become international in scope, because it was remote – so equally accessible (or equally inaccessible) to all Greeks. The only nearby state of any size and importance was Elis, two days' journey on foot to the north, and Elis did not really start to develop as a state until well into the eighth century BCE, and remained relatively insignificant in international terms for many decades. The town of Pisa was closer (and hence Olympia is sometimes called 'Pisa' by the poets), but was even smaller, little more than a farm town. Otherwise, Olympia was cut off by the Peloponnesian mountains to the east and by the sea to the west.

For the majority of visitors, getting to Olympia was easier by boat than by foot or wagon or mule. The journey by sea was perfectly feasible for everyone, especially for the Greeks of Magna Graecia – Sicily and southern Italy – but it took some effort. The nearby shoreline had long stretches of sand where boats could easily be beached,* and from there it was only a matter of a few miles overland to Olympia. There were one or two small harbours as well. In ancient times the coastline was much closer to Olympia than it is today. It was possible, therefore, for light vessels to approach the site by sailing some way up the Alpheus, which flowed into the Ionian Sea west of Olympia.

---

* Ancient ships could not stay long in the water. It was necessary to allow the oarsmen to rest, to dry out the insides of the ships, and to kill the destructive teredo 'worm' (actually a kind of wood-boring mollusc).

Over many centuries, changes in the courses of the rivers have washed away some of the site of Olympia. Earthquakes added to the destruction, and recent tests have raised the possibility that a tsunami in the middle of the sixth century CE completed the job. Whatever the causes, the site became covered with several metres of silt. Olympia was effectively lost. Of course, locals knew there was something there, as floods or their ploughs turned up shards of pottery, broken roof tiles and fragments of old stonework, but the site was officially 'discovered' by the English explorer and antiquary Richard Chandler in 1766, in the course of an expedition funded by the Society of Dilettanti in London. The society was dedicated to the study of Greek and Roman art.

The first excavations were undertaken by the French in 1829 (under the direction of the architect Guillaume-Abel Blouet, who later completed the Arc de Triomphe in Paris), but they did little more than partially uncover the temple of Zeus. The French expedition to the Peloponnese was actually a military expedition, which was accompanied by Blouet and his colleagues, as well as by other scientists and artists. And the reason for the French expedition was that the Greeks were in the process of freeing themselves by revolution from almost 400 years of Turkish rule. The Greeks were not doing a very good job of it on their own, since their freedom fighters tended to fight among themselves; they were helped not just by the French, but also by the British and Russians, as well as by many individual 'Philhellenes' ('lovers of Greece') from as far afield as the United States of America. The most famous of these Philhellenes was Lord Byron of England, who put his considerable fame as an aristocrat and a best-selling poet to the service of raising money and support for the revolutionary cause, before dying of disease in the course of the war in Missolonghi in central Greece. The Greek War of

Independence broke out in 1821, but it was not until 1832 that independence was formally won.

The rush of nationalistic pride that followed independence encouraged the new Greek nation to take better care of its antiquities and, as well as creating their own archaeological service, the Greeks gave permission to the archaeological institutes of the European superpowers, and later America, to conduct proper, meticulous, scientific digs. This coincided with the time when the great museums were being created in London, Berlin, Paris and elsewhere, as the collections of curios and antiquities that had been hoarded by individual aristocratic households were amalgamated and given to the nations concerned. These museums were symbols of national power, and their collections were seen as evidence of their countries' reach into far-flung, obscure parts of the world.

The excavation of Olympia was granted, after lengthy negotiations, to the Germans, and work began in 1875 under the auspices of the German Archaeological Institute. For the first time a clear division of the spoils was laid out: all excavated finds would remain the property of Greece (so that they would not be taken back to Germany, as had usually been the case in earlier years), while the Germans had the right to publish the finds and the results of excavation. The first archaeological campaign continued until 1881; the second, coinciding in part with the German wartime occupation of Greece, lasted from 1936 until 1941; and the third began in 1952 and has continued every year since. The site being very large, and archaeology being painstaking work, the excavations are still ongoing; even the gymnasium has yet to be fully uncovered.

The heart of the Olympic complex was the Altis, a 'grove' sacred to Zeus, whose worship began there in the eleventh century BCE, and one of whose oracles was located there. We know very little about the working of this oracle, which seems to have specialized in military prophecies; its fame was eclipsed by that central Greek institution, Apollo's oracle at Delphi. Games began at Olympia in some form in the eighth century BCE and continued until the end of the fourth century CE, when, as pagan rites, they were closed by the Christian emperor of Rome, Theodosius the Great. Over these eleven centuries, as well as a colossal fifth-century-BCE temple of Zeus, many other structures were built in the Altis, and then developed and redeveloped, so that the modern visitor is faced with a perplexing mass of stone-strewn zones, making a good guidebook or guide essential. The original guidebook was written by Pausanias of Magnesia-by-Sipylus (in Asia Minor, modern Turkey) in the second century CE. He travelled all over southern Greece (in those days the Roman province of Achaia), penning descriptions of the monuments that he saw, and he lingered long at Olympia. The first archaeologists frequently referred to his work to help them identify what they were uncovering.

The crowded nature of the Altis today echoes the busy nature of the ancient Olympic festival, as thousands of spectators, peddlers, slaves (labourers, or accompanying their masters), poets, entertainers, athletes, priests, fortune-tellers, state representatives and Olympic officials wound their way among the sacred and secular buildings, and statues of gods and athletes. The Olympic festival was attended by a true cross-section of Greek society. An inscription survives from the Roman period, from Beroea in Macedon, commemorating the eight visits to Olympia by a baker called Caecilis.[3] There were booths selling food and souvenirs to festival-goers; the rivers nearby were an adequate source of water,

George Gordon, 6th Baron Byron (1788–1824), who used his fame as an A-list celebrity to support the cause of Greek freedom. By Thomas Phillips, 1813.

and, in addition, wells were dug before each festival.

The earliest stadia, the first two that were built, lay partly inside the Altis, but by the third quarter of the fourth century BCE the precinct was becoming too crowded with buildings, and a new stadium was built just to the east of the Altis – the third in what would prove to be a sequence of five constructed over the centuries. Since the fourth and fifth refurbishments introduced only minor changes and improvements, it is essentially the third stadium that we see today. It is an awesome structure, whose capacity testifies to the enormous popularity of the ancient festival: over 40,000 spectators could be seated on its banked slopes – as many as Chelsea Football Club's famous Stamford Bridge stadium, or as Wrigley Field in Chicago, home of the Cubs. Only a few seats were made of stone and elevated: one set, on the south side of the track, was for the umpires and a few dignitaries; the other, opposite them, was for the local priestess of Demeter. She was appointed to her post at the beginning of the festival, but it is not clear what part she played in the festivities; scholars tend to think that her presence there was something of a hangover from the past. Athletes approached the stadium through a vaulted passageway, built towards the end of the fourth century.

For the sake of experiencing the thrill of attending the greatest religious festival in the Greek world, spectators were prepared to put up not only with weeks of hard travel, but also, once they had arrived at Olympia, with intense heat and unsanitary conditions, with sleeping in the open, with being constantly jostled by crowds, and with dodging thieves. Tents were pitched and huts constructed outside the sacred Altis, even some distance away (apart from considerations of overcrowding, there was also the important matter of avoiding polluting the Altis with the smell of human waste), and it is likely that visitors from the same Greek states occupied the same patches of ground at successive festivals. The level ground south of the hippodrome (horse track), around the River Alpheus, was popular. There was probably also some kind of hierarchy, in that the rich occupied the slopes of the surrounding hills, where their tents could catch breezes, while poorer visitors sweltered and sweated lower down.

The rich also had proper tents or pavilions, and were attended by their slaves, while the poor simply sheltered under a piece of canvas slung between branches or propped up on poles, or slept out in the open. The games took place, after all, at the height of summer, when the weather was so hot that Thales of Miletus, we hear, one of the Seven Sages of Greece, died of heatstroke at Olympia during the festival of 548.[4] The contestants themselves were accommodated in rooms attached to the gymnasium – or, at least, they were from the third century onwards; before that they had to camp out like everyone else. The first hotel, with several dining rooms, was built towards the end of the fourth century BCE, but it was a high-end facility, with accommodation only for a tiny percentage of the visitors. Its construction was paid for by a wealthy benefactor called Leonidas, from the island of Naxos.

GREEKNESS

Whether they were rich or poor, and whether they came from one of the few great states or one of the many that were small and obscure, everyone at Olympia recognized themselves as kin. The games were an affirmation of Greekness that was particularly important for those visiting from overseas or the fringes of the Greek world. When the fifth-century-BCE historian Herodotus of Halicarnassus said that one of the things that bound all Greeks together, wherever they lived, was their common sanctuaries and festivals, he was thinking of the Olympic festival and others like it.[5] A shared religious festival such as the Olympics gave the

Greeks a chance to recognize their cultural unity – even though, as we shall see, it often did little to disguise their political disunity.

Greeks lived not just in the country that is nowadays called 'Greece', but also in separate states all over the Mediterranean and Black Sea coastlines. From about the middle of the fifth century onwards, judges were appointed at Olympia – they were called the *Hellanodikai*, the 'judges of the Greeks' – and one of their jobs was to make sure that all contestants were genuinely Greek, full citizens of their states (in particular, not slaves) and of good standing in their states. Greekness remained a prerequisite for several centuries, until from the end of the third century BCE the rule was obsequiously bent for Romans, the new masters of the Mediterranean world (though in fact they entered only the equestrian events, and left the rest to Greeks).

The usual exclusions and divisions of Greek society applied to those who took part in and watched the games: the athletes in the games were all men;* slaves were allowed to compete only as proxies for their masters in the equestrian events; and married women (with the single exception of the priestess of Demeter) and non-Greeks were not allowed even to watch, although they were permitted to do so at some other festivals. Since women married not long after puberty, only very young women – adolescent girls, effectively – were allowed in. Philostratus, writing in the third century CE, tells a story which had sprung up in ancient times and which illustrates the prohibitions against women at the games. A woman called Pherenice travelled from the island of Rhodes to accompany her son Peisirhodus, who was competing in the games as a boxer. She disguised herself as a man in order to gain admittance to the trainers' enclosure, but when Peisirhodus won, she leapt for joy – and in so doing disarranged her clothes

---

* Female games, especially for young unmarried women, took place in a number of locations across Greece, including Olympia, and we will return to this topic later (see pp. 127–30).

and was discovered. From then on, the judges had the right to ask even the trainers to strip.[6]

THE TEMPLE OF ZEUS

For all its remoteness, the sanctuary developed from simple beginnings into one of the most magnificent locations in the ancient Mediterranean. Dominant in the Altis was the great temple of Zeus, the largest temple in the entire Peloponnese. It was built in the second quarter of the fifth century BCE by the people of Elis to commemorate their final defeat of the Arcadian people of Pisa, with whom they had been disputing control of Olympia for at least two centuries.* The temple was so large that it would have been too expensive to make it out of marble, which was not locally available; a cheaper fossil-bearing limestone was used, which was then plastered over to give the appearance of marble.

By the last third of the fifth century, the temple housed one of the acknowledged wonders of the ancient world, the 13-metre-high (43 ft) statue of Zeus seated on his throne, the creation of the celebrated sculptor and architect Pheidias of Athens. The materials, gold and ivory on a wooden frame, were chosen not just for their splendour, but also because if such a large statue had been made from the traditional materials, hollowed bronze or stone, it would have been far too heavy. In Pheidias' vision, Zeus was majestic, but not fierce; he was Zeus *Nikēphoros*, Zeus the bringer of victory.

It was Pheidias' success in designing and executing the gold-and-ivory statue of Athena for the new Parthenon in Athens in

---

* This was not the only time that control of wealthy and prestigious Olympia was a cause of war: see p. 168.

the early 430s that led to his being commissioned to make the Zeus statue as well. He had proved his ability to work on a colossal scale. Astonishingly, thanks to the fortuitous discoveries of a cup with his name inscribed on it and fragments of clay moulds for the statue's drapery, Pheidias' workshop at Olympia has been identified, buried beneath a later Christian church. It is possible that these pieces survived for so long because the workshop was turned into a kind of museum once the statue became famous. The workshop, which was aligned with the temple, was designed as a replica of the interior room of the temple where the statue was to be housed, so that Pheidias could work with the exact dimensions. The statue was then disassembled in the workshop and reassembled in the temple.

The statue was still in existence in the second century CE, when Pausanias saw it during his tour of Greece:

> The god, who is made out of gold and ivory, is seated on a throne. On his head is a wreath made to look like sprays of olive. On his right hand he bears a figure of Victory, which is also made out of gold and ivory, and has both a fillet and a wreath on its head. In the god's left hand is a sceptre, adorned with every metal imaginable. There is a bird perched on the sceptre – an eagle. The god's sandals are also of gold, and so is his robe, which is decorated with figures and lily flowers. The throne is embellished with gold, precious stones, ebony and ivory; it has painted figures on it and relief sculptures. There are four Victories, portrayed as dancing women, one at each foot of the throne.[7]

The statue survived at Olympia until the end of the fourth century CE, when it was removed to Constantinople, the 'second Rome' and capital of the eastern Roman empire. It was lost in a massive conflagration that destroyed much of the city centre in 475 CE.

When the athletes first gathered in the Altis, they did so beside the temple, and the painted sculptures that adorned it –

The statue of Zeus, by Pheidias of Athens, was a major attraction for tourists and pilgrims alike, and was considered one of the wonders of the world.

now beautifully displayed at eye level in the Olympia museum, though the paintwork has long gone – showed them models of heroism and glory, designed to inspire them to fulfil the old Homeric ideal of 'striving always to be the best, superior to others'.[8] The sculptures depicted the labours of Heracles, a model of strength and virility. They showed how the local hero Pelops (after whom the whole Peloponnese – the 'island of Pelops' – is named) won his legendary chariot race against Oenomaus not by cheating (as one version of the story has it; see p. 40), but by divine favour, the message being that men could be inspired by the gods to win; Pelops in legend was a mortal man who became more than human – a 'hero' in the Greek religious sense – and was therefore a suitable role model for the athletes of Olympia. And the sculptures also showed the battle of the human Lapiths against the savage Centaurs – a battle in which the Lapiths are portrayed as athletes, especially wrestlers. The humans defeated the beasts by their superior discipline – an obvious message for ambitious athletes.

THE GLORIOUS ALTIS

Olympia was not sacred to Zeus alone. By early in the third century BCE the Altis also contained important temples to Zeus' wife Hera (the earliest surviving temple in Greece, dating from the early sixth century BCE) and Rhea, the mother of the gods; an ancient shrine to Pelops; an oracular shrine of Zeus; the beautiful but notorious Philippeium (in which Philip II of Macedon, the father of Alexander the Great, portrayed himself and his family as though they were gods); majestic administrative buildings; colonnades for shade, shelter and shopping; treasuries filled with valuable dedications by successful athletes and states; a huge gymnasium for the athletes to train in; the Hotel Leonidas; and a number of other grand buildings.

Zeus' altar, on open ground in the Altis, was not a structure of any kind, but was made up entirely of a huge mound of ash and debris, solidified by the fat of the repeated animal sacrifices that were carried out not only during the quadrennial festival, but at regular intervals in between; the site was not deserted between Olympics and was frequently visited by pilgrims. In the time of the Greek travel writer Pausanias, who wrote his *Description of Greece* in the second century CE, the cone of ash was 7 metres (23 ft) high, with a circumference at its base of 38 metres (125 ft); it was stepped, to allow access to the top. For all its size and unusual nature, the altar was not unique: there was another like it at nearby Mount Lycaeum, another site where games were held in honour of Zeus. The altar at Olympia marked the spot where Zeus was said to have hurled his thunderbolt when laying claim to the Altis – perhaps taking it over from other, earlier deities.

Blood sacrifices took place every day of the Olympic festival, culminating in a 'hecatomb'. This word means literally 'the sacrifice of a hundred oxen', but was also used to designate any large number of sacrificial victims, short of a hundred, but still constituting an impressive and expensive sacrifice. The beasts were generally provided by states and wealthy individuals, rather than by the organizers of the games. The hecatomb was a major and messy event: every ox had to be slaughtered, one after another, and then carved up; the joints were either cooked on the spot or distributed to individuals for cooking and sharing with their friends and retainers. Eating together was the typical aftermath of animal sacrifices in Greece, and the sacrifice and the feast were the joyous consummation of the festival. There was no room for vegetarians – though Athenaeus of Naucratis in Egypt, writing in the second century CE, tells the unlikely story that the philosopher–mystic Empedocles of Acragas (himself from

a family of Olympic victors), a follower of Pythagoras in this respect, fashioned a tasty ox out of barley-dough and honey and made that his contribution to the festival sacrifice.[9]

Then there were the statues; only a number of pedestals survive now, scattered here and there around the Altis, but originally they were everywhere, lining every pathway, commemorating victories in athletics and war. Olympia was a museum or hall of fame as well as a sanctuary and athletic venue. The statues, usually about life size, might be free-standing figures in a heroic pose or one that suited the athletic event they had won; the equestrian statues were particularly impressive, the largest of them consisting of an entire four-horse chariot group in bronze. Towering over all was Paeonius of Mende's *Nikē* (Victory), dedicated at the end of the 420s BCE by the people of Messenia under dramatic wartime circumstances – a defeat of the usually invincible Spartans at the battle of Sphacteria in 425. Perched on top of a column 9 metres (30 ft) tall, it depicted Victory swooping down on the Altis.* Victory was what Olympia was all about, but she was fleet of foot. Her impressive height was closely rivalled early in the third century by gilded statues of Ptolemy II of Egypt and his sister-wife Arsinoe, standing on top of pillars over 8 metres (26 ft) tall in front of one of the main colonnades.

The statues were put up either by the victor himself or by his home town, once permission had been obtained from the Olympic officials. They were in effect votive statues; if victory is given by the god, then the victor might dedicate a statue as a way of thanking the god. The practice of commissioning a sculptor to commemorate victory in this way began early in the sixth century, and at first the statues would have struck spectators as

---

* Paeonius was a famous sculptor in his day, and produced pieces especially for Olympia, but little of his work survives. The remains of the statue, Victory's body outlined by flowing drapery, can be seen in the Olympia Archaeological Museum.

quite extraordinary, because making likenesses of living human beings was new. Olympia was largely responsible for bringing the European tradition of portraiture into being. Not every statue accurately reproduced the victor's features and physique; many were idealized portraits with only the attached inscription picking out personal details. But still, the practice of sculpting a likeness of a living man began there, or was given a major boost, with the commissioning of victory statues. That is why, even centuries later, the Greco-Macedonian kings of Egypt and Syria, despite the luxury and sophistication of their courts, still liked to be depicted heroically nude. The naked athletic body became the archetype of virility, and athletic poses always gave sculptors the chance to show off their mastery.

Next to the vaulted entrance to the stadium were a number of bronze statues of Zeus, on whose pedestals were inscribed the names of those who had tried to cheat in the games: identified here were competitors who had attempted to trip their fellow runners, to bribe judges or other contestants, to persuade their rivals to hold back or to represent a state of which they were not citizens. We also hear of athletes being cursed – for instance, 'If Eutychian wrestles, let him fall and make a fool of himself' – and presumably that would have counted as cheating if the tablet on which the curse had been written had come to the judges' attention.[10] But such curses were generally buried in the ground, in order to activate the gods of the underworld to carry out their mission. There were very few of these statues of cheats – their erection seems to have been a temporary phase in the fourth century – and the considerable costs of raising them were paid for by the cheat or his native city. Earlier and later, cheats had to put up with no more than being publicly humiliated on the spot with a flogging, and paying a hefty fine.

In the stadium itself, planted all over the banked slopes on which the spectators sat, were stakes of wood hung with armour

taken from some enemy in battle, often made to look vaguely humanoid. These battlefield trophies were erected here because Olympia was the principal place for celebration of victory and therefore a favoured location for the dedication of victory spoils. There was an unwritten rule that a tenth of the profits of war should be dedicated to the gods, and this was one way in which Olympia became extremely wealthy. The trophies overlooked the athletes as they competed in the stadium, and afforded a little shade for a few spectators.

Over the course of time, the buildings at Olympia became truly impressive. Vast sums of money were spent on embellishing the site, and running the games too must have been a very expensive business. Money came from the Elean public treasury (including revenues from renting out the stadium as farmland between festivals), but also from voluntary or obligatory benefactions by the rich (a standard practice among the Greeks, since they lacked regular income-taxation systems). Despite the fact that there appears to have been no admission charge for spectators at Olympia, it is likely that the festival at least broke even, as a result of all the donations made by visitors. Even if there was a financial shortfall, the Eleans probably did not mind, because by running the games they gained prestige – symbolic capital, if not capital in the form of hard cash.

The battle between centaurs and humans, on the western pediment of the temple of Zeus, represented the quelling of an opponent by disciplined athleticism.

Origins

The modern Olympics – the games were resurrected in 1896 – are peripatetic: a different city hosts the games every four years. The ancient Olympics, for all of their existence, were held in just the one place, Olympia, and I have suggested that it was felt to be a suitable venue because its remoteness made it, at least potentially, neutral ground, where competitors could meet as equals. But how did the games start? Here we need to distinguish reality from the stories the Greeks themselves told in answer to this question. They were perennially fascinated by cultural origins, and came up with a range of possibilities for the Olympics. To the Greek way of thinking, an institution as important as the Olympics must have had the most auspicious of beginnings. As with other aspects of their culture, they looked back to the gods, or to the great heroes of myth and legend, to explain how the games began.

MYTH

According to one story, recounted by Pausanias and deriving, he says, from local antiquaries, the gods themselves chose Olympia as a site of contest. In this version, it was at Olympia that Zeus wrestled his father, Cronus, for the right to be king of the gods; one of the Dactyls (the deities who raised the infant Zeus) initiated the foot races as contests between himself and his brothers; while Apollo beat swift Hermes at running and even Ares, the god of war, at boxing. But, since the gods plainly no longer walked the earth, this divine institution of the games (which some went so far as to date to 1581 BCE) was in time forgotten, and the games therefore needed to be revived later.[1]

In another account,[2] the games were instituted by the divine hero Heracles. In order to commemorate the successful completion of one of his twelve labours, the cleaning of the Augean stables in nearby Elis, he cleared the Altis, defined its boundaries, and instituted the first games in honour of Zeus. The length of the stadium (close to 192 metres, or 210 yards) was determined, it was said, either by the distance Heracles could sprint without drawing a breath, or by measuring 600 lengths of his foot.

The story of Heracles' institution of the games was widely accepted as fact. The sixth-century philosopher and mathematician Pythagoras is said to have believed it so completely that he used it as a basis for calculation.[3] All the major stadia of Greece were 600 feet long (a distance known as a 'stade', hence our word 'stadium'), but what counted as a foot varied. A stade length at Olympia was a little over 192 metres, while at Corinth it was 165 metres. So, having calculated Heracles' foot size, Pythagoras used that as a basis for calculating his height.* The philosopher concluded, pedantically, with the observation that 'Heracles was taller than other men by the same factor as that by which the stadium at Olympia is longer than all the others that have been laid out with the same number of feet.'

Another tale, almost as widely disseminated as the Heracles version of the festival's origins, looked back to the mythical chariot race between Pelops and Oenomaus.[4] Pelops wanted to marry Hippodamia (the 'tamer of horses'), the daughter of Oenomaus, and inherit Oenomaus' throne as king of western Arcadia, but Oenomaus had ruled that, in order to do so, a suitor must first defeat him in a chariot race. Suitors' races are common in Greek myth and legend, but this one was of heroic proportions, from the western to the eastern side of the Peloponnese. The skulls of the young men who had tried and failed to meet Oenomaus'

---

* The ratio between foot size and height was held to be fairly constant; the Greeks even used to make appointments by saying 'Meet you at ten-foot time', because it was assumed that when my shadow was ten lengths of my feet, yours would be ten of yours.

challenge adorned the lintel of the king's palace. Pelops, however, was determined to succeed.

From this point, there are two diverging versions of the story. In the most familiar version, Pelops won by cheating. He suborned Oenomaus' stable hand to sabotage the king's chariot so that a wheel fell off during the race and Oenomaus was dragged to his death. In the other version, Pelops won by divine favour; the god Poseidon, who loved Pelops, gave him winged horses with which he defeated Oenomaus.*

Pelops, then, founded the games to commemorate his victory over Oenomaus. The trouble with this idea is that it runs counter to the belief, accepted by almost all Greeks, that the earliest games consisted only of running races, and that the equestrian events were introduced later (chariot racing was the first to make an appearance, in 680 BCE). So a story centring on a chariot race cannot have been the original foundation myth; it must have arisen later, after chariot racing became a fixture at the games. Since Oenomaus was a king of Pisa, perhaps Pelops' victory over him represented the first victory of Elis over Pisa for control of the games in the sixth century. But, whatever the date at which the story arose, it took hold of the popular imagination: Pausanias records that in his day there were many artefacts at Olympia that harked back to it, not least the barrow and grove of trees inside the Altis that marked the supposed tomb of Pelops. Another mound, next the hippodrome, was said to be haunted by the ghost of Oenomaus, and horses shied away from it.

It would not have worried the Greeks to have a contradictory set of myths explaining the origins of the Olympic festival. Their myths were like that – a mass of interlocking stories, constantly

---

* In the previous chapter, I suggested (following a minority of scholars) that the sculptures of the east pediment of the temple of Zeus at Olympia reflected this latter version of the story. It would not make much sense to have the Olympic athletes inspired by a version in which the hero is a cheat and a murderer.

The death of Oenomaus in the common version of the story of the chariot race between him and Pelops for the hand of Hippodamia.

Burney del.

Scott sc.

refined and added to and altered. The important thing was that every one of these myths was represented by some structure or sacred spot within the Altis. The Altis was bound together by its myths; every time the games were held, their mythical origins resonated in the minds of contestants and spectators.

LEGEND

Moving from myth to the realm of legend – that is, to the realm of allegedly historical persons – we come across the shadowy figure of Iphitus, an early king of Elis, who was thought, in conjunction with Lycurgus, the legendary lawgiver of Sparta, and a king of Pisa called Cleisthenes, to have revived the games after the original festival, inaugurated by the gods themselves, had lapsed. They are said to have instituted the games because the Greeks were fighting among themselves and they asked the Delphic oracle what they could do to put an end to these conflicts. The oracle replied, in effect, that war should be sublimated in the pseudo-war of athletic competition, and that a truce should be established for the duration of the games. So Iphitus revived the games and established the truce (see pp. 88–9); at first, the games involved only the sprint, but other running events, and then other kinds of contests, were introduced over time, until the games had their familiar form and structure.

By far the most influential book by an ancient scholar on the origins of the Olympics was the *Olympic Victors*, written by the polymath Hippias of Elis at the end of the fifth century BCE. He may have been commissioned to write the book by his home town. Nothing of this work has survived (apart from one scrap of papyrus), but it was widely influential, so that we can infer some of its content from its reflection in later writers such as Aristotle, who brought Hippias' lists of Olympic victors up to date, to include the results of later games. It was Hippias, in all likelihood, who perpetuated or came up with the idea that the games had been revived by Iphitus, Lycurgus and Cleisthenes. And it was probably Hippias who formalized the practice of identifying individual Olympic festivals by the names of the winner of the stade race. Thus the games of 200 BCE were 'the games at which Pyrrhias of Aetolia won the stade race'.

Most famously, it is to Hippias that we owe the traditional date for the first Olympic festival: 776 BCE. It is, in fact, impossible to be sure exactly when the games began, but the chief importance of the date is that it remained, thanks to Hippias, the start of the Olympiad dating system, whereby a new Olympiad began every fifth year This gave the Greeks their basic system of reckoning time, so that they would say, for instance, that the Battle of Marathon took place in the third year of the 72nd Olympiad – or, to us, 490 BCE. It was a pan-Greek system, designed to supersede and supplement all the particular calendars of particular states, which tended to indicate years by specifying which senior politician was then in office (as in 'the year in which so-and-so was Archon of Athens').

We have no idea how Hippias arrived at the date of 776 BCE, but he was not far off, as we shall see. His conclusion is likely to have been based on original research, involving information assembled from various different sources. Other scholars came up with alternative dates: in the third century BCE, for instance, another polymath, Eratosthenes of Cyrene, proposed 884 as the date for the start of the Olympics. According to his system, 776 was merely the date when the victor lists began to be drawn up. Nevertheless, Hippias' identification of 776 as the date of the first Olympics held its ground and retained its ascendancy throughout the history of the ancient Olympics.

Modern scholars have been no less anxious than their ancient counterparts to identify the original purpose of the games, which led to their foundation. Many of them have noted the Greek practice of organizing games to commemorate the death of an important individual, and have posited a funerary basis for the games at Olympia. The most famous such funeral games are those of Patroclus, described in the twenty-third book of Homer's *Iliad*, written around 700 BCE, which involved a chariot race, boxing, wrestling, running, fighting in armour, throwing a weight, archery and javelin throwing.

There is a good deal of comparative anthropological data to support the idea that the games had some such commemorative function. Premodern societies around the world have used competition to choose a successor to a dead king, or to propitiate his spirit by entertaining him, or to reintegrate their communities after the loss of a leader. In ancient Greece itself, annual funerary games were instituted in the northern city of Amphipolis after the death in 422 BCE, during the Peloponnesian War, of the man they claimed as their founder, the Spartan general Brasidas.[5] Two of the other great athletic festivals of ancient Greece, the Isthmian and the Nemean games, were associated with funeral cults. At Olympia, however, there is really no plausible candidate for the hero in whose honour the games were instituted. Pelops is the only choice, but, as we have already seen, the chariot race for which he was famous was a later addition to the Olympic programme, and therefore games consisting of running races are unlikely to have been founded for his death. Also, while the ancient Greeks themselves knew of the link between funerals and games, there is no evidence that they applied it to the Olympics. The Olympic games were an affirmation of life, but not necessarily in the context of death.

Some scholars therefore look elsewhere. It is common around the world for rites of passage to require physical exertion from the people being initiated, and this practice was not unknown in ancient Greece. The athletic festival for unmarried girls that took place at Olympia (which we will look at later) was certainly initiatory in character. So perhaps the games started as a rite of passage for men. The trouble is that there are no real grounds for applying this theory to the ancient Olympics; there is no trace of such an idea either in Greek writing about the games, or in the rituals that accompanied them.[6]

Equally speculative is the idea that the games evolved from pre- or post-hunt rituals.[7] In Stone Age times, hunters would meet and perform certain rituals in order to ensure that the hunt had the desired outcome. Sacrifices and feasting simulated the aftermath of a successful hunt and propitiated the gods so that they would not thwart future hunts. When animals became domesticated, they became easier to kill, and hunting therefore became less fundamental to human survival. According to this theory, athletics developed because it involved the equivalent expenditure of energy that in earlier days had been devoted to hunting. There are certainly connections between hunting and some ancient Olympic events – running, hurling a stone (discus) or javelin, horse riding – but Stone Age practices will have died out centuries before the inauguration of the Olympic festival, and are unlikely to have been at all influential on it. Another version of this theory argues that running was an aspect of the ceremonies *following* a successful hunt, and suggests that in prehistoric times Olympia was a popular location for members of the elite to meet and hunt wild cattle.[8]

These theories are all sophisticated guesses. My own view is much simpler – that the games evolved out of the natural competitiveness of the Greek elite. It seems plausible that, given the desire to 'strive always to be the best, superior to others' (in the

Homeric sentiment quoted in the previous chapter), the Greeks found more and more ways to try to prove their superiority to others, starting with simple running races and going on from there. There exists a completely natural desire, evident in children from their earliest years, to try to outdo one's peers by physical means. Who can reach the end of the field first? Who can throw the stone furthest? Who is the best at wrestling? This view does not rule out any of the more sophisticated theories I have just outlined, but it may be sufficient on its own.

The question remains why Olympia in particular became a site for athletics. The answer may lie in the presence there of the oracle of Zeus, which had long been consulted by those seeking advice on military matters. Victors in battle may have returned to Olympia after their success to dedicate some of their spoils there, and to celebrate their victory with athletic competition. What began as a spontaneous outpouring of energy in the company of friends and rivals became gradually more structured and formalized.

ARCHAEOLOGICAL EVIDENCE

Faced with this profusion of myths and legends, one is tempted to agree with the Greek geographer Strabo, who said, towards the end of the first century BCE: 'One should ignore the ancient stories about the founding of the sanctuary and the establishment of the games… There are many versions of these stories, and none of them is worthy of credence.'[9] Fortunately, help is at hand in the form of evidence derived from archaeology; we are literally grounded by it.[10]

Archaeological evidence reveals that people first lived at Olympia around 1400 BCE, but that this settlement was abandoned

Bronze tripods-plus-cauldrons were costly, and so made
suitable dedications at Olympia for Greek aristocrats
to commemorate victory and show off their status.

and forgotten. Visitors returned to the site in the late eleventh century, when the worship of Zeus and other deities at Olympia began. It was always an elite site, as is revealed by the presence here of dedicatory items made of metal, which could have been afforded only by the rich. Its remoteness was part of its appeal to such men; by dedicating valuables there, they were showing not only that they could afford to pay for such items and dispose of them by dedication, but also that they had the means and the time to leave their homes and communities and undertake the long journey to Olympia.

The material evidence revealed by excavation shows a clear development: the site was used at first exclusively by people from nearby in the western Peloponnese, especially Elis, Messenia and Arcadia, with a smaller number coming from Argos, the greatest of the Peloponnesian states at the time. By the end of the eighth century, Spartan presence was firmly established as well, but there was still no participation by states from further afield. There is no evidence of permanent settlement, so it is likely that at this time the site was being used only for occasional meetings and perhaps already for a periodically recurring festival.

At this stage, it is impossible to tell whether or not the worship of Zeus at Olympia (if indeed at this point he was the supreme god there, which is not certain) involved athletic contests as well as sacrifices and dedications, but it makes sense to think that it did. Bronze tripods were commonly dedicated at Olympia in these early decades (some of a colossal size, the equivalent in value of a dozen strong oxen), and in Homer's *Iliad* bronze tripods were sometimes prizes in athletic contests, though they had other uses as well. By the end of the eighth century, or early in the seventh, wells were being dug in Olympia. An area of the Altis was levelled as a proto-stadium, and the Hill of Cronus that overlooks it was terraced, presumably for spectators, turning the whole Altis into a kind of theatre. Moreover, in a major feat of

This seventh-century griffin head, originally an ornament for a tripod, gives an impression of how large, expensive and magnificent these bronze vessels might be.

engineering, the River Cladeus was permanently diverted away from the Altis. We can safely say, therefore, that the athletic side of the festival was in place by the early seventh century, and there is no reason not to push it back a few decades; these large-scale works of construction would not have taken place unless the need for them had already become well established.

So Hippias and Greek tradition were surprisingly accurate. It is very likely that some kind of athletic activity began to take place at a periodic festival held at Olympia in the second half of the eighth century, and that for a while it consisted of simple running races. Cult buildings and monuments began to be erected late in the seventh century, and the site was then further developed over the centuries. By the beginning of the seventh century, visitors and athletes from beyond the Peloponnese, and especially from Magna Graecia, were coming to Olympia. Eventually, they would arrive here from every corner of the Greek and Roman worlds. Not surprisingly, athletes from the Peloponnese and from elsewhere on the Greek mainland were the dominant presence at Olympia; but participants came from wherever there were Greek settlements: from Egypt and North Africa, from Syria, Asia Minor and Sicily.

THE COMPETITIVE ETHOS

Greeks belonging to the wealth-and-warrior elite invented competitive athletics, but why did they do so? It seems that participation in international athletic competitions was just one of a number of strategies by which the elite kept themselves distinct from the rest. They were a leisured elite; they did not have to work for a living, but lived off the labour of others, and they made it clear that they were a breed apart from such lowly, uncultured others. At one point in Homer's *Odyssey*, when Odysseus turns down an invitation to take part in an athletic contest, the man who has invited him sneers. 'Yes, you don't look like a man who competes for prizes,' he says. 'You seem more like a trader, with his mind fixed only on profit.'[11]

The elite of the Archaic period of Greek history (c.750–480 BCE) were those with wealth based on their possession of the best farmland or pasturage, and on the best trade contacts abroad. As Greek states coalesced or re-coalesced in the eighth century, members of this elite began to take responsibility for the governance and defence of their states. Their authority came not just from the economic and military power that they wielded, but also from their leadership of local religious cults and from symbolic strategies such as conspicuous benefactions to the community.

In the Archaic period all the states we know of were ruled by small groups of these aristocrats, who often intermarried exclusively among themselves or took as wives the daughters of their peers abroad, so as not to allow wealth and power to accrue to families of lesser status. None of these groups was entirely closed, however, since some families were bound to fail economically, or to fail to produce a living son to continue their line; they did not have an absolute monopoly on landownership or trade, and new fortunes were made which elevated outsiders into their ranks. Status was never entirely a given, but was always subject to negotiation and merit. And the potential for sporting achievement to burnish an individual's reputation was one of the factors that made athletics increasingly important. It was not unknown for men to consider themselves worthy to rule their states just because they had been Olympic victors.

Members of the Greek elite, wherever in the Mediterranean world they hailed from, adopted an extraordinary lifestyle which emphasized their superiority to other men and therefore reinforced their fitness to rule. They created long lineages for themselves, going back to the gods and heroes of old. They were given to ostentatious displays of wealth. They continued to bear arms in the streets, even after civic defence had become the responsibility of the state, rather than individuals, and even after personal disputes had become matters for resolution by the law courts, not by vendetta. They distinguished themselves by hunting, athletics and feasting, and by travelling abroad – pursuits that require leisure and money. They took to wearing long, flowing garments of expensive material in the eastern fashion – clothing that was imported and bought rather than made by the household's womenfolk, as was usual. They wore their hair long and elaborately coiffured; they wore gold jewellery and perfume, and spent as much of their leisure time as they could enjoying wine and song, as though to emphasize that they did not have to work.

International festivals such as the one at Olympia were celebrations of aristocratic class solidarity and occasions for elite display and rivalry. Only aristocrats could afford the kind of physical training that would turn themselves and their sons into competitive athletes. Only they could afford to take time off to train for and participate in athletic events; contestants at Olympia had to swear that they had been in training for the past ten months, and were obliged to spend a whole month immediately before the festival training under the eyes of the Olympic officials. They were also the only ones who could afford to breed horses, which were used for racing and warfare, not for traction or transport. The philosopher Plato agreed: 'To devote your life to winning at Delphi or Olympia keeps you far too busy to attend to other tasks.'[12]

The only way less wealthy competitors could get a look-in was if they were financed by a wealthy patron or by the state. In 480 and 472, for instance, the people of Argos used their common resources to enter the prestigious four-horse chariot race at the Olympics, which they won, defeating all the individual aristocratic contestants. The Athenian Panathenaea games, which were held every four years from the second quarter of the sixth century BCE, involved a very large number of local athletes: not all of these can have come from the ranks of the super-rich; some of them must have been subsidized by private sponsors.

There is evidence for less well-off athletes taking part in the Olympics as well: the philosopher Aristotle, writing around 330 BCE, records an epigram for an Olympic victor – we do not know his name – which reads: 'In times past, on my shoulders a rough yoke, I used to carry fish from Argos to Tegea.' Then we have an inscription from Ephesus, dating to around 300, recording the indirect sponsorship by the state of a promising young athlete called Athenodorus – indirect because the proposal before the executive branch of the city was to grant citizenship to those individuals who had financed his training. And on a papyrus from a few decades later, from Ptolemaic Egypt, there survives a letter in which the private sponsorship of an athlete is discussed.[13] This is sparse evidence, but the practice certainly increased in later years. Gradually, over the long history of the games, men from lower down the social scale began to take part, but they remained few in number, and the culture of Olympia remained elitist.

The equestrian events were certainly monopolized by the rich. Greece is short of productive land, and one horse eats as much barley as a household of five or six people. Ownership of a horse was therefore a sign of social distinction, like owning a Ferrari today. A lot of upper-class Greek names included elements of *hippos*, the Greek word for 'horse': Hippias, Hipposthenes, Callippus, Philippus and so on. Even if a poorer athlete could make such a name for himself as a track-and-field athlete at local festivals that he could move up to the international games, he was still excluded from the equestrian events. It was claimed by the son of the super-rich and super-arrogant Alcibiades of Athens at the end of the fifth century that his father had refused to take part in anything but equestrian events 'because he knew that some

In terms of thrills and spills, the four-horse chariot race was the supreme event of the ancient Olympics.

track-and-field athletes were low born, from small states and uncultured'.[14]

Elite Greeks, then, especially in the Archaic period, were keen to separate themselves from the lower born and mingle only in one another's company. And when they met, they invariably competed. At the drinking parties known as symposia, for instance, they did not just drink and sing, but tried to outdrink one another and to invent wittier songs than their companions. They played competitive games, such as flicking the dregs from their cups at a target. They took part in public musical competitions as well, and when drama was invented in Athens, early in the fifth century, the playwrights took part in a competitive festival. Even plays as great as Aeschylus' *Oresteia* trilogy, Sophocles' *King Oedipus*, and Euripides' *Hippolytus* were written not just to entertain an audience, but to win a prize. Medical doctors competed against one another in public debates, actors were awarded prizes for their performances, potters boasted of their superiority to other potters, some cities held contests for sculptors. Here and there in the Greek world, there were beauty contests for boys, girls or men. The following exchange from one of the conversations of the philosopher Socrates, recorded by Xenophon of Athens, encapsulates the Greek attitude towards competition:

> 'Tell me, Charmides,' said Socrates. 'Supposing there was
> somebody capable of winning at the major athletic competitions
> so as to gain honour for himself and enhance his country's
> reputation in Greece, and supposing that he refused to compete,
> what sort of man would you think he was?'
> 'Obviously, I'd regard him as soft and a coward.'[15]

No other ancient society appears to have been so competitive that it needed to develop athletic contests. There is little evidence of competitive sport in the ancient Near East, at least until that part of the world began to be influenced by Greek customs in the Hellenistic period (323–30 BCE). There are many depictions of wrestling and stick fighting from Old Kingdom Egypt as far back as the third millennium BCE; the Egyptians seem to have used it for military training, but there is no sign that they went so far as to organize athletic meetings. Closer to Greece, there are two depictions of boxers from the southern Aegean island of Thera (modern Santorini), which was culturally Cretan at the time. One is on a heavily restored fresco, dating from about 1600 BCE, and the other on a cup made about fifty years later. The 'Boxer Rhyton', as the drinking cup is called, shows young men boxing, wrestling and bull leaping, but since bull leaping is unlikely to have been a competitive sport, and was, in all likelihood, a test of courage used as a rite of passage from youth to adulthood, then perhaps boxing and wrestling also served initiatory rather than competitive functions in the Minoan culture of Crete and Thera.

Ancient Greece was not a single place. In the Classical period (479–323 BCE) there were over 1,000 autonomous city states, great and small, all over the Mediterranean and the Black Sea, and they rarely united. Even when the Persians invaded Greece early in the fifth century, only thirty-one states united to resist them, while the rest either sided with the Persians (willingly or unwillingly) or stayed neutral. The competitiveness of individual Greeks reflected the competitiveness of their states, which vied with their neighbours for territory and dominance. In any case, the elite commonly *were* the state, so even in international affairs and warfare, they felt they were competing with their peers. Their competitiveness was recognized: in democratic states, which exercised more authority over individuals, members of the elite were encouraged to channel their violence and rivalries into athletics, rather than allowing such energies to disrupt society in any way. The invention of athletics, and the ensuing appearance of many venues for games, were natural outgrowths of elite Greek competitiveness.

overleaf
The eastern pediment of the temple of Zeus. Pelops
and Oenomaus flank Zeus in the centre, as he
supervises their oaths prior to their chariot race.

Sport and society
in ancient Greece

The Olympic festival was the earliest and the greatest athletic festival of ancient Greece, but by the second quarter of the sixth century BCE four other major athletic festivals had come into being, at Delphi, Nemea, Corinth and Athens. There were plenty of local festivals too, and some which attracted more limited international attendance, but these were the only five that were truly international – until the third century, which saw the beginning of a long-lasting trend for cities around the Greek world (which had been hugely expanded by the eastern conquests of Alexander the Great) to bid for international status for their own major athletic festivals. In 279, for instance, Ptolemy II, king of Egypt, sent envoys all around the Greek world, requesting recognition that the Ptolemaea, the new games he had instituted in honour of his dead father, be granted Olympic status. Holding such games was profitable as well as prestigious, and by the time the Romans ruled the Mediterranean, from the middle of the second century BCE, the Greek world teemed with major athletic festivals.

The second-oldest international festival was the one at Delphi, called the Pythia (Python was perhaps an old name for the district of Delphi). This festival, instituted around 650 and sacred to Apollo, originally emphasized musical competition, since music was one of Apollo's special provinces, but it underwent a major overhaul early in the sixth century (in 586) and became largely a regular athletic meeting along Olympic lines. A few years later, in 580, the Isthmian games, sacred to Poseidon, were established on the Isthmus near Corinth; then in 573 the Nemean games were founded at nearby Nemea (for Zeus) and in 566 the Greater Panathenaea at Athens (for Athena). Other games were founded at much the same time – the Pythia of Sicyon, for example – but these four joined the Olympics as the most important and popular festivals.

In the early sixth century athletics in Greece moved from

being a marginal pursuit to the mainstream, and all five festivals quickly became truly international, attracting competitors from all over the Greek world. The Olympics were at that time just beginning to become more widely international, and the establishment of the other four festivals hugely accelerated that process. In a very short space of time, all five festivals became central to the lives and lifestyles of the Greek elite. The fact that Archaic Greece – a small and sparsely populated place – could support five magnificent athletic festivals is a measure of elite Greek competitiveness, and a sign that athletics had been taken up by the sub-elite as well, the next-wealthiest layer of society, made up largely of successful farmers, traders and craftsmen. Athletic success was a sure way to climb the social ladder.

THE FESTIVAL CIRCUIT

Four out of these five festivals were carefully coordinated with one another as a formal festival circuit. The Panathenaea was excluded, for unknown reasons.* As for the others, in any four-year period (an Olympiad), games were held at Olympia in July/August of the first year; at Delphi in July/August of the third year; at Nemea (or Argos, where the Nemean games were located for certain stretches of their history) in August of the second and fourth years; and on the Isthmus near Corinth in April of the second and fourth years.

The Pythia at Delphi was considered the second-most

---

* Perhaps it was too closely associated with a particular city, Athens, rather than being on supposedly more neutral ground – though the plausibility of this theory is eroded somewhat by the fact that all the games were held under the auspices of one Greek state or another, with political consequences for Olympia that we will look at later.

prestigious festival after the Olympics. Since it took place at the same time of year as the Olympics, it was in effect an intercalated Olympics, a filler between occurrences of the Olympic festival. But prestige is not everything, and in time the Isthmian games, being more easily accessible, grew to rival the Olympics for popularity, until the festival became 'the meeting place of Asia and Greece'.[1] In 196 BCE, when the Roman general Titus Quinctius Flamininus wanted the largest possible audience for his announcement of a regime change in Greece, he chose the Isthmian games.

The athletic events at these festivals did not differ much from those at Olympia. Winning at any of these festivals brought enormous prestige and pride – so imagine what it was like for a man to win his event at each of the four games within a single circuit, or even at all six games, winning twice at Nemea and the Isthmus. Such a man was a *periodonikēs*, a circuit victor, and there was no higher status for a living athlete – like winning all four Grand Slam tournaments in tennis. The achievement became even more difficult after 27 BCE, when the Roman emperor Augustus added the Actia to the circuit. Games, sacred to Apollo, had long been held at the mouth of the Gulf of Ambracia on the northwest coast of Greece, but Augustus upgraded them and added them to the circuit to commemorate his final victory in the Roman civil wars at the Battle of Actium in 31 BCE. The Actia were held every four years in September, in the second year of an Olympiad.

THE CIRCUIT IN THE 72ND OLYMPIAD

OLYMPIAD AND YEAR	PLACE	TIME
72.1	Olympia	July/August 492
72.2	Nemea	August/September 491
	Isthmus	April/May 490
72.3	Delphi	July/August 490
72.4	Nemea	August/September 489
	Isthmus	April/May 488
73.1	Olympia	July/August 488

The contestants preserved the sacredness of these festivals by making leaf crowns the prizes, rather than anything valuable; hence they are known as the 'crown games'. When the Actia were added to the circuit, they too were made crown games. At Olympia, the crown was of olive; it was made from twigs cut with a golden knife from a sacred olive tree within the Altis by a boy with two living parents – which was unusual enough in those days to count as a sign of Fortune's blessing. At Delphi, the crown was of bay; at Nemea of wild celery (which is bendy enough to be made into a crown); and at the Isthmus of pine or wild celery, at different times.

The historian Herodotus imagined a conversation between some Greeks from Arcadia and a Persian grandee who came from a culture with no athletic tradition. When the Persian asked the Arcadians what was happening in Greece at the time, the summer of 480 BCE, 'they replied that the Greeks were celebrating the Olympic festival, and watching athletic competitions and horse races. The Persian next asked what the usual reward was for winning, and they told him about the garland of olive that was given as a prize.' At this, the Persian expostulated with his commander-in-chief: 'Mardonius, what sort of men are these you have brought us to fight? They make excellence rather than money the reason for a contest!'[2] But Herodotus' opposition between excellence and money is too stark, because a victor at any of these four games would certainly gain in material terms. The Greek words betray this: an athlete, *athlētēs*, is literally a competitor for a prize, *athlon*. Money was perhaps not as important as glory for most competitors, who were already rich enough, but it added value to the enterprise.

A victor could look forward to being rewarded in his home town, and not just with intangible honours. On top of generous amounts of cash, he might be dined for life at the state's expense, or be made exempt from certain taxes; he might even translate his success into senior political posts and military commands. In Sparta, with its bizarre militarized constitution, Olympic victors were accorded the privilege of fighting in battle alongside the kings (Sparta had two of them) and forming their bodyguard. By the Roman period, when there were very many athletic festivals around the Mediterranean world and further east, Olympic victors could command huge appearance fees.

These rewards were of considerable value, and many more were available at local games around the Greek world. The value of the prizes meant that they did not go uncriticized. The poet Xenophanes of Colophon listed early in the fifth century the typical rewards received by a victorious athlete and then said: 'But he doesn't deserve them as much as I do. My intelligence is more important than the strength of men or horses. Custom here makes no sense; it is not right to rank strength above intelligence.'[3] And intellectuals as eminent as Socrates and Isocrates of Athens echoed Xenophanes' complaint, which became a commonplace of Greek literature. At his trial in 399, the philosopher Socrates suggested that an appropriate punishment for his alleged impiety would be for him to be dined for life at public expense. This was a typical reward for a victor in the circuit games, and Socrates argued that his work had been far more valuable to the city:

> So what reward is appropriate for a poor man who has been a
> benefactor of the city and needs leisure time to help you?
> Athenians, there is nothing more appropriate for such a man
> than to be fed in the Prytaneum, and this is far more suitable
> for him than for any of you who wins the horse race at Olympia,
> or the two-horse or four-horse chariot race. An Olympic victor
> makes you considered happy, but I make you actually be happy;
> and he has no lack of food, whereas I do.[4]

The judges disagreed, and he was condemned to death.

Sometimes a victor would take matters into his own hands

and attempt to seize the reward he believed was his due. In 636, an aristocrat named Cylon tried to make himself sole ruler of Athens on the strength of his being an Olympic laureate from an earlier games. He launched his coup at the time of the Olympic games because he knew that his peers and rivals would be away at the festival, but when they returned they put an end to his endeavour.[5] Two hundred and twenty years later, the notorious Alcibiades was suspected of wanting to do the same. In the Olympics of 416, he had achieved a unique success. It was not just that he had unprecedentedly entered no fewer than seven teams in the four-horse chariot race – something no one had ever achieved or even come near to before – four of which had finished first, second, fourth and seventh, but also that, in doing so, he had ended a long run of Spartan victories in this prestigious event, at a time when Athens was at war with Sparta. Back in Athens, he celebrated his success by commissioning the playwright Euripides to compose a celebratory epigram and famous painters to glorify his victories. Entering twenty-eight horses (twenty-four, in fact, because one team was borrowed) was indeed a kingly gesture, and the Athenians were right to fear Alcibiades' ambitions. Within three years he had fled Athens to avoid trial.

Personal glory accruing from Olympic victory was an influential fact of Greek aristocratic life for much of the sixth century. This was reflected in the erecting of statues at Olympia to commemorate individual victories (see p. 30), a practice which began at the time of the establishment of the circuit. By the end of the century, however, state-built 'treasuries' were being constructed to house dedications at Olympia (on a special terrace under the Hill of Cronus), indicating perhaps that states were now attempting to curb individual pride by appropriating some of the glory for themselves.

Athletes went to the games on their own initiative; they were

not selected or, generally, financed by their states, and indeed athletes competed with as much rivalry against their fellow citizens as they did against everyone else. But it looks as though athletes were, from the end of the sixth century, thought of as in some sense representing their states. When they were introduced at the games, it was by name and state; this would normally be the athlete's birth state, but we do hear of athletes hiring themselves out, so to speak, to other states. Despite the arrival of state-built treasuries, however, individual merit could still be celebrated by commissioning a victory statue from a sculptor, and poets such as Pindar and Simonides of Ceos were on hand at all the games of the circuit to compose commemorative poems. Pindar, naturally, claimed that song was a far superior way to commemorate victory than a lifeless statue.[6] These poets would presumably approach the victors afterwards, or make themselves available to be approached. Perhaps sculptors did the same.

THE GYMNASIUM

By the middle of the sixth century BCE, then, a great deal more effort and commitment was being put into athletic activities. Anyone who wanted to win glory had to become more professional in his training and preparation. Every town of any size therefore now supported at least one gymnasium and a wrestling ground (*palaistra*), which was sometimes attached to the gymnasium, for men and boys to practise and stay fit. Over the course of time, because athletics became so fundamental an aspect of Greek identity, the very presence of a gymnasium would define a city as being Greek or Hellenized. When in the second century a small town called Tyriaeum in Phrygia (in Asia Minor) wanted to raise its status to that of a city, it asked the local king for permission not just to develop its own laws and administer itself, but also to build a gymnasium.[7] In Palestine, during the same century, the rebellion of the Maccabees against the Seleucid dynasty (which started in 167 BCE and would result ultimately in the establishment of the first Jewish state) began as a reaction against reformist Jews who wanted to abandon their faith and take on Greek culture – symbolized, among other things, by the building of a gymnasium in Jerusalem.[8] In Ptolemaic Egypt, one way to refer to Greeks in official documents was 'the people of the gymnasium'.

Gymnasium culture was the same all over the Greek world. A gymnasium was a place where men and boys exercised naked – that is what the word means – but it was a multi-use facility, designed also for recreation, meetings with friends and the physical education and military training of boys. Gymnasia were built at public expense (often with the help of benefactions by wealthy citizens) and maintained by men who were appointed by the state or who volunteered for the job for the sake of its prestige, despite the huge expenses it entailed (especially on oil, heating and ensuring a constant supply of running water). They were usually built on the edges of towns, where there was sufficient space, level ground and a nearby water source. Independent wrestling grounds, however – those that were not attached to gymnasia – tended to be privately owned.

A fairly basic gymnasium of the fifth or fourth century had two running tracks, one enclosed and one in the open, where all the track-and-field events were practised. It was sure to have a *palaistra*, a rectangular structure with an interior courtyard where the combat sports were practised. The courtyard was surrounded by a colonnade that provided shade, seating and corridor access to meeting rooms, hot and cold bathing rooms, and rooms where athletes changed, prepared themselves and were rubbed down with oil and cleaned after exercising. The gymnasium at Olympia

overleaf
One side of the wrestling ground within the gymnasium, where contestants at Olympia practised their events, prepared themselves on the day, bathed, socialized and slept.

had nineteen such rooms. A gymnasium was, in other words, a very substantial structure, and often one of the most splendid buildings in a town.

Gymnasia consumed a great deal of olive oil. This was used partly as fuel for lighting purposes, but mainly for rubbing into athletes' bodies before they exercised. Afterwards, before the athlete washed himself with a sponge, the oil and sweat and dust was scraped off his body with an instrument known as a strigil – a curved scraper with a groove for collecting the dirty oil (which was, oddly, held to have medicinal properties). A set consisting of a strigil and an oil flask was an athlete's signature equipment. Oiling the body served as pre-exercise massage (much as nowadays we stretch our muscles before exercising), and it apparently helps to conserve body moisture, but it was not done just for these limited practical purposes. Nor was the point, for a wrestler, to make his body slippery; wrestlers were obliged to sprinkle dust over their bodies after they had oiled themselves, to allow their opponents to get a grip. They tossed the dust into the air and stood under it, so as to get even coverage all over their bodies.

The main reason for oiling the body was to display oneself, fit and gleaming, to one's peers and admirers. The value of athletics for toning the body is a constant theme in Greek literature. Pindar often celebrated the beauty of the younger victors for whom he wrote songs. Of one, called Epharmostus, he says: 'What a shout went up as he paraded around, young and noble in achievement as in looks!' Centuries later, a Greek orator of the first century CE, Dio Chrysostom, said of the boxer Melancomas of Caria: 'No matter how many boys and men were exercising, when Melancomas stripped no one looked at anyone else.'[9] Melancomas was such a skilled defensive boxer that he had retained his good looks.

The Athenian philosopher Plato occasionally imagined his mentor Socrates starting up one of his conversations while seated in the colonnade of a palaestra.* His dialogue *Charmides*, for example, takes place in the palaestra of Taureas in Athens. Socrates calls young Charmides over, because he is interested in the beautiful boys of Athens – beautiful in mind as well as body. Charmides' arrival 'caused a lot of laughter, because each of us who were sitting down immediately began to push his neighbour, to make room for Charmides to sit next to himself, until we forced the man sitting at one end to stand up and dumped the one at the other end on the ground to the side.' Then 'the entire crowd of visitors to the palaestra began to gather around us,' to enjoy the treat of hearing Socrates' quizzing of the teenager.¹⁰

As well as being a place for physical exercise, then, a gymnasium or palaestra was a place of recreation (for meeting friends, or for listening to philosophers or a recital of Homer's poetry) and a homosocial and homoerotic environment. It was a place for stretching not just the body, but the heart and the mind as well. The gods of the gymnasium, whose statues graced the courtyards and corridors, were Heracles (strength), Eros (sexuality) and Hermes (intellectual interaction). 'Happy the lover', sang Theognis of Megara in the sixth century, 'who exercises in the gymnasium and then spends the rest of the day at home in bed with a beautiful boy.'¹¹ Plato theorized that it was physical contact in the gymnasium that caused a boy to reciprocate the love of an older man.¹²

Many gymnasia, however, took care to separate the youngest boys from adults, to minimize the opportunities for underage homosexual encounters. The younger and passive partner in the kind of temporary, almost ritualized homosexual relationship that was common among the Greek elite was a teenager, between the ages of puberty and beard growth, and some states made it illegal

---

* Plato's own school, the famous Academy, was named after the Athenian gymnasium where he did much of his teaching.

to made advances to such a young boy.[13] The main reason why boys were present in gymnasia, from the age of seven onwards, was because some of their schooling took place there. Their physical education was supervised by a *paidotribēs*, a 'trainer', and 'physical education' meant practising the standard athletic events, not just as an end in itself, but also as a way of instilling courage and developing physical beauty.

Gymnasia were frequented largely by elite boys and men from the leisured class; everyone else was busy working. The anonymous author of an anti-democratic pamphlet written some time towards the end of the fifth century in Athens accused the common people of Athens of being jealous of those who were able to make use of gymnasia 'because they know that they cannot afford to engage in these activities'.[14] A law dating from the early sixth century, attributed to the Athenian lawgiver Solon, forbade slaves from exercising or being naked in gymnasia, its purpose being to restrict the chances of sexual attraction between slaves and free boys.[15] A long inscription survives from Beroea in Macedon, from early in the second century BCE, detailing the complex regulations for the gymnasium – who was allowed in, who was allowed to exercise naked, the duties of the gymnasium staff, the levels of fines for misconduct and so on. Shopkeepers, prostitutes, slaves and freed slaves were excluded by the snobbish elite; madmen, homosexuals, drunks and the disabled were also debarred.[16]

TRAINING

There were tensions inherent in the notion of self-improvement that the discipline of athletic training entailed. An aristocrat was supposed to maintain his position in society thanks to his inherited qualities. That went for his athletic ability too – but having his abilities improved by trainers obviously contradicted this ideal. We see here the clash between amateurism and professionalism which has also haunted the revived, modern Olympic games. In ancient times it was most noticeable in the fact that the owners of the horses that took part in the equestrian events rarely rode the horses or drove the chariots themselves; they had trained slaves do it instead. In order to preserve at least the pretence of the amateur, Homeric ideal, these highly trained slaves were consistently ignored when it came to praising the winners of equestrian events, in favour of the wealthy owners of the horses they rode.

At some point, the oath that contestants had to swear at Olympia began to include the guarantee that they had trained assiduously for ten months. This was largely to ensure that athletes were as fit and skilled as they could be, so that the best possible competition would be laid on. The demand for athletes to reach a peak of physical fitness for the games, and the concomitant need to follow a strict training regime, led to the emergence of professional trainers. They were often retired athletes, and the most successful of them became wealthy and famous. There were several statues at Olympia of trainers. Melesias of Athens, who specialized in training boys, had at least thirty victors to his credit early in the fifth century.[17]

Working either out of a gymnasium or as personal trainers, they taught the techniques appropriate to particular events, treated injuries, and saw to it that their charges were generally fit and healthy. Most of their teaching of technique has been lost, even though handbooks were written, but we know something of the kind of regimen they prescribed: plenty of rest and massage, and a bulky diet that included far more meat than was usual for ancient Greeks. Charmis of Sparta, however, the Olympic sprint winner in 668, was said – although it does not seem very likely –

overleaf
The gymnasium was so large that it contained both indoor and outdoor full-length running tracks for practice and friendly competition.

to have eaten exclusively figs. Some recommended that athletes conserve energy by avoiding sex while in training, a myth that would turn out to have a very long life. The athlete Cleitomachus of Thebes used to leave the room if anyone so much as mentioned sex, and could not abide to see dogs copulating in public.[18]

We hear of trainers shouting out advice from the ringside.[19] Glaucus of Carystus demonstrated his natural strength one day on the family farm by beating a ploughshare back into shape with his bare hands. His father took him to the Olympics of 520, and despite Glaucus' inexperience he made it through to the finals of the boxing. But by then he was so badly hurt that everyone expected him to give up – until his father suggested: 'Son! The one you used on the ploughshare!' But advice could be psychological too, designed to boost a contestant's morale. The trainer of one flagging boxer told his man that his beloved would marry only an Olympic victor. The recipient of this message, suitably inspired, duly defeated the reigning Olympic champion – though, sad to say, the trainer was lying and the boxer did not get the girl. Another trainer pointed out to his exhausted charge that a man could win eternal fame even by dying at Olympia. And that was exactly what the unfortunate athlete proceeded to do.

Philostratus, who wrote *On Athletic Exercise* in the third century CE, informs us of a four-day training cycle that was popular in his day. Day one was given over to 'preparation' and involved a number of short, sharp exercises – perhaps pyramid training of some sort. Day two, 'concentration', was devoted to all-out effort, intended to exhaust the athlete. Day three was for 'relaxation', recovery from the previous day's efforts, and on day four, the day of 'moderation', the athlete practised the techniques peculiar to his event. Wrestlers would wrestle one another, and even practised a form of mud wrestling, training themselves in the ability to get a secure purchase on a difficult opponent; boxers practised by shadow boxing or light sparring or with a punch bag; runners practised their starts. The cycle then began again on the next day. Philostratus objects that this rigid regime takes no account of the athlete's particular personality, but the system bears some resemblance to interval training today, with its variation between low- and high-intensity workouts.

Cross-training was rare; training was usually rehearsing one's event, even in extreme ways: Amesinas of Barce in North Africa, Olympic wrestling champion in 460 BCE, was said to practise by wrestling a bull. We hear of a boxer, Teisander of Naxos in Sicily, who kept himself fit by swimming long distances, and the second-century CE physician Galen, whose work underlay the practice of medicine for the best part of 1,500 years, recommended the virtues of ball games (none of which was an event at the major festivals) and some light weightlifting. Wrestlers might do a little light boxing to keep the muscles loose. Athletes were expected to maintain overall fitness by an outdoors lifestyle and hunting.[20]

The Stoic sage Epictetus, writing at the end of the first century CE, summarized what every athlete knows:

> 'I want to win at Olympia,' you say, but you should consider the corollaries and consequences of this desire… You have to be disciplined, follow a strict diet, give up desserts, train under compulsion at fixed times in extremes of heat and cold. You must not drink cold water, nor wine at other than the appropriate times; you must put yourself in your trainer's hands just as you would submit to a doctor.[21]

NUDITY

At many festivals, including Olympia, the athletes performed naked in the track-and-field and heavy events (boxing, wrestling, and pankration); they also exercised naked in the gymnasium. In equestrian events the riders usually wore clothes – not for reasons of modesty or comfort, but because the training they undertook did not allow them to develop bodies worth showing off to the world. There was probably another reason too. The elite owners did not themselves ride the horses they entered; in the days before saddles and stirrups it was dangerous and uncomfortable, so, with very rare exceptions, they got slaves to do it for them – and to the Greek way of thinking no one would want to see a slave's naked body. The same went for chariot racing, with its attendant dangers.

Nudity was unique to Greek athletics and, within the Greek world, unique to athletics; elsewhere public nudity was a source of shame, not pride. Why, then, did the Greeks adopt this practice? Originally athletes had worn loincloths, but these had fallen into disuse by the middle of the seventh century, when we have the earliest unambiguous evidence on a painted vase. The stories the Greeks told about why they practised naked athletics are plainly no more than guesses. Two of them, for instance, told of how a runner's loincloth accidentally fell off. In one version,[22] the athlete found that he could run faster without it, but in the other the loose loincloth tripped him up; he died of his wounds, and the Olympic officials decreed that from then on all athletes should be unclothed. The Romans were on the whole more prudish than the Greeks, and it is unlikely that the naked Olympics survived the imposition of Roman rule on Greece in the second century BCE. Roman athletes wore a breech-cloth.

There are painted vases in existence, and literary accounts (albeit from people writing many centuries after the event), showing that some athletes tied their penises back against their bodies by means of a thong. The Greeks, for whom *kuōn* ('dog') was one of many slang words for the penis, called the thong a *kunodesmion* ('dog-leash'). But the reason for this practice is unclear. Scholars generally say that it would have lessened the

After competing, athletes scraped the oil, dust and sweat off their bodies with a strigil, which would originally have been held in this statue's right hand.

discomfort of naked athletics, but this is questionable at best. The penis is not the part of the male genitalia that needs securing for the sake of comfort.

Besides, it is not certain that athletes actually *competed* with their penises restrained in this way. Who would run with a tight leather thong around his waist? What wrestler would give an opponent a chance to lock his hand inside the thong? The purpose of the practice, which was not unique to athletes, might have been to symbolize sexual restraint, or to signal to admirers that their advances would not be welcome. Perhaps one of the purposes of nudity in general was to display one's self-control – to show that, even when surrounded by beautiful naked bodies, a man might not get aroused.

The principal aim of athletic nudity was to display a fine, well-muscled body, gleaming with olive oil. The elite of Greece were, in the phrase coined in fifth-century Athens, 'the beautiful and the good', and the assumption that a fine exterior was a reflection of virtuous character was rarely questioned. The Olympic games were a summation of the aristocratic ideals of physical skill, beauty and strength, of competition, of publicly displayed piety and of honour freely or grudgingly given by one's peers. The important point was that your adversaries were your peers. When Alexander the Great, who was apparently no mean sprinter, was asked if he would compete in the Olympics, he said: 'Only if my rivals are kings.'

Nudity, tying back the penis and the application of olive oil were adopted for ritual and aesthetic purposes rather than practical and performance-enhancing ones. The underlying message was probably: 'What you see is what you get. I am as I appear to be.' Nudity might perhaps have acted as a leveller, since whatever class of society they come from all naked men are equal – but, as we have seen, for many decades after the introduction of nudity the gymnasia and the international games were monopolized by the rich. Aristotle even claims that athletic nudity was one of the ways in which the rich distinguished themselves from others.[23] More critically, as was the case in the gymnasium, homoerotic overtones were also present in the stadium. In this respect, the Olympic games were gymnasia expanded onto an international stage.

The Olympic festival

The timing of the Olympic festival was arranged in such a way that a full moon – the second after the summer solstice, which occurs between 20 and 22 June – would fall on the central day, the third of the five-day festival. This is, of course, a very hot time of year in Greece – heat was one of the acknowledged discomforts of the festival – but there was little agricultural activity going on then, and since almost everyone in those days made a living from agriculture, they had some spare time. The grain had already been gathered in, figs and grapes would not be ripe for another few weeks, and the olive harvest would not start until December. Slaves could keep things ticking over at home. This was also considered the safest time of the year to sail, and most visitors to the games came by boat.

THE SACRED TRUCE

Before the actual festival, there were certain preliminaries. Above all, there was the announcement of the sacred truce. Even though everyone knew when the festival was going to take place, officials still travelled the length and breadth of the Greek world well in advance, announcing its start and proclaiming the truce that preceded the games. The origins of the sacred truce may lie in warfare. After an ancient Greek battle, it was usual for a truce to be arranged so that the two sides could collect their dead and bury them. If they also honoured their dead in some way – for instance, by impromptu games – the truce would have covered that too. The Olympic officials may have borrowed the idea of a truce from there.

The truce was originally one month long, but this was extended to two and even three months once people began coming to the games from far afield. Contrary to popular belief, it did not ban warfare entirely: its only proscription was that for the duration no one was allowed to attack Elis itself, the city which put on the games; in fact, for the best part of two centuries, until the very end of the fifth century, because of its management of the games Elis as a whole was considered sacred land that was not to be attacked at any time of year, not just during the truce. And, on the whole, the Eleans tried to avoid entanglement in Greek wars.

Otherwise, inter-Greek fighting might still go on during the truce; the sequence of modern Olympiads has twice been interrupted by warfare (the First and Second World Wars), but that was not the case for their ancient counterpart. The games continued, for instance, throughout the Peloponnesian War of 431–404, in which almost all Greek states were involved. We have already seen how Cylon tried to seize power in Athens during an Olympic festival; the coup failed, but there was never any suggestion that Cylon had breached the Olympic truce.

What the truce did was, in effect, classify the thousands who wanted to attend the festival as pilgrims, under divine protection, so that they were not to be harmed or hindered from travelling there. It is not clear how this protection was enforced, other than by superstition; the truce was supposed to be guaranteed by the god Apollo at Delphi. The truce did not always work – in fact, in 364 BCE there was fighting in Olympia itself during the festival – but violation of the truce was liable to a hefty fine, and even Philip II of Macedon, the most powerful man in Europe at the time, was once required to recompense an Athenian who had been robbed by some of Philip's soldiers as he was on his way to Olympia.[1]

Other festivals, not just the Olympics, were protected by sacred truces, but they all became redundant in the second century BCE. By then warfare among Greeks had died down of its own accord, as the Romans kept the peace, the *pax romana*, throughout the Mediterranean world.

Another important preliminary to the Olympic games was the appointment of the judges, the *Hellanodikai*. At first, there were only two, but the number was raised to nine in 400 BCE and in 392 to ten – three for the equestrian events, three for the foot races, three for the combat events and the pentathlon (discus, long jump, javelin, sprint and wrestling), and one president. The judges were citizens of Elis, chosen by lot from a preselected short list of candidates, and were appointed well in advance to ensure that they had acquired the relevant expertise by the time the festival began. They had to be well off, because they were not paid for their efforts; indeed, the role required them to contribute money as well as time. The judges were instructed by an Elean committee called the Guardians of the Law, who assessed the rule book, decided if any changes were to be made, and instructed the judges accordingly; these guardians were presumably former judges themselves. For the duration of their term, the judges used one of the main colonnades of Elis as their daytime office, and slept in a separate building in the centre of town. They did this not just to mark themselves as special, but so that they did not have to commute from their rural estates.

By at least the end of the fourth century, when the number of contestants was large enough to warrant it, all of the athletes were required to stay in Elis (which, like an Olympic Village today, had both training and dormitory facilities) for a month before the games. Late arrivals for registration were automatically disqualified unless they had a cast-iron excuse. Having assured officials that they had trained assiduously for the previous ten months, contestants then had to undertake a full month's training in Elis. This proves that, even as late as the third century BCE, participation in the games remained the preserve of the rich and the well funded; only individuals such as these could afford take so much time off work, pay their trainers, and absorb the other costs arising from their attendance at the games.

During this month, the judges had various tasks to perform. They had to register the contestants, supervise them at their training, make sure that they knew the rules and would play fair, and eject those who were not true Greeks. The athletes practised their events under the rigorous eyes of the judges, and the fascinated eyes of some early-arriving fans. It was a period of 'friendly' games, if you like – but it was the end of the road for some. Another of the judges' jobs was weeding out the unfit and incompetent, so as to guarantee a high standard of performance – pleasing to both gods and spectators – when the games proper began. Contestants put themselves forward for the games on their own initiative, and were not required to take part in a 'qualifying round' before they arrived at Olympia; so the judges were, effectively, deciding who qualified and who did not. It was not unknown for only a single contestant to be left after this weeding-out process; under such circumstances, he was automatically declared the winner of his event. The Greeks called this a 'dustless' victory (*akoniti*). On one occasion, the judges cancelled the wrestling altogether, presumably on the grounds that there were no competent competitors.

The judges also had to assign contestants to their age classes. At Olympia, there were only two classes, men and boys, but at some of the other crown games there was an intermediate class of 'youths', competitors in their late teens. The boys' events were introduced at Olympia in 632, according to Hippias' reckoning. A contestant seems to have been classified as an adult if he was aged eighteen or over, and in exceptional cases a man might still be competing in his forties: Hipposthenes of Sparta, for instance, won the wrestling in five consecutive Olympics between 624 and 608, and Milo of Croton may have been Olympic wrestling champion at six successive games from 540 to 520. Men who

were even older could enter a chariot team or a horse for an event, because they had slaves to do the dangerous work. Those who found their lust for glory unsated after their retirement from physical participation in the games often turned to these equestrian events, if they could afford to do so, in an attempt to prolong their careers as victors.

We hear nothing about a fixed minimum age for boys. The criterion for letting them participate was probably physique rather than age; ancient Greeks had no birth certificates. In a case dating from the fourth century, a boy was so big and strong that the judges wanted to classify him as a man, until they were persuaded not to do so by Agesilaus II of Sparta; in 368 the boys' stade race was won by a twelve-year-old.[2] Another of the judges' tasks was to classify the horses for the equestrian events – to decide whether an animal should race as a colt or a horse.

For the games themselves, the judges wore expensive purple-dyed clothes, the clothing of kings, and carried forked sticks. They had the power to expel athletes from the games, to fine them or to punish them on the spot for cheating or lying or infringing the rules (if, for instance, a wrestler tried to break his opponent's fingers); as the Olympic police force, they were accompanied by whip-bearers. It is remarkable that the judges were allowed to use such a humiliating form of punishment on high-born athletes; flogging was usually reserved for slaves, or for boys at school.

It was the judges' job to organize the draw, decide the winners, arrange the prize-giving ceremony and give permission for the erection of statues. If the entrants for the stade race were too numerous for the twenty lanes that the stadium at Olympia could accommodate, the judges would have to arrange preliminary heats; and then for the final the lanes were decided by lot. For the heavy events and the pentathlon the draw was decided by lot. If there was an odd number of contestants for any of the events that required paired competitors, someone was awarded a bye; a bye

At Olympia, athletes competed either as boys or as men. Here we see a boy preparing for the long jump – note his hand weights.

was also awarded, naturally enough, if one's opponent withdrew. In the event of a dead heat or a draw, no one was awarded the olive wreath, but it was dedicated to Zeus instead and that particular race or event was declared 'sacred'.

The judges were, of course, supposed to be impartial, and their swearing an oath to that effect was the official starting moment of the games. They swore to judge fairly, to accept no bribes and not to divulge any information about particular athletes to which they were privy. These were Elean judges, however, and Eleans were allowed to take part in the games as contestants. The Greeks were aware that this situation might test the judges' impartiality:

> It is said that the Eleans, who took their management of the Olympic games very seriously, sent envoys to Amasis [an Egyptian pharaoh of legendary wisdom] to ask him how they could be sure to conduct the games with the utmost fairness, and he replied: 'If no Elean citizen takes part in the games.'[3]

But in 396 just such a controversy occurred. Two of the three judges awarded first place in the stade race to an Elean, Eupolemus, while the third awarded it to Leo of Ambracia. Leo claimed that Eupolemus had bribed the two judges and appealed to the Olympic Council, a branch of the Elean government consisting of fifty senior men who were responsible for the day-to-day running of Olympia and acted as an appeals court in such cases. The judges were fined, but their judgement was not overturned: victory still went to Eupolemus.

Generally, the judges seem to have been scrupulously fair. From 372, however, it was made illegal for them to compete in the equestrian events while serving as judges. The percentage of Elean wins at Olympia was not markedly greater than that at other games, especially if we allow for 'home-town advantage'. Even after the Roman conquest of Greece, the judges treated their Roman masters no differently from how they treated Greeks –

Praxiteles' famous fourth-century 'Hermes with the Infant Dionysus' was originally displayed in the temple of Hera at Olympia, where it was rediscovered in 1877.

except when Emperor Nero insisted on taking part in the games. First, he had the games – not just the Olympics, but all the games of the circuit – delayed so that they would coincide with his tour of Greece in 67 CE and he could have himself acclaimed a circuit victor. At least that gave the Olympic officials time to build an enormous villa for him, whose remains are still standing today. Then, at Olympia, even though he fell from his chariot – which he insisted on driving himself – and was unable to complete the race, he was still crowned the victor. He was also crowned for the musical competition he instituted at the festival, despite the acknowledged awfulness of his singing. After his death the following year, his name was erased from the list of victors and the judges were censured and compelled to return the money Nero had given them in thanks for their generosity.

THE FIRST DAY

Shortly before the start of the games, the site itself had to be prepared. A fascinating inscription has survived from Delphi, pertaining to the Pythian games, that shows the variety of jobs that needed doing and what the labourers were paid.[4] At Olympia, wells were sunk and springs were cleared of debris and undergrowth; buildings were spruced up; roads and bridges repaired; the stadium and hippodrome dug up to loosen the soil, weeds and stones removed, and the surfaces rolled flat and sprinkled with white sand. Ground was dug up and loosened for the jumpers also, and turning posts for the running races were erected. Lanes for the runners were marked with whitewash. Finally, the starting mechanism (*hysplēx*) was checked; introduced in the last quarter of the fourth century, it caused a rope, stretched in front of the starting line at about knee-level, to drop, releasing the runners and preventing false starts (a floggable offence).

On the day before the start of the games, the contestants processed from Elis to Olympia. The procession was instigated in the sixth century. It is not clear exactly what route it took, but the distance involved would have been over 35 miles (50 km). Once the athletes had assembled, the judges made an announcement:

> If you have worked so as to be worthy of going to Olympia, if you have done nothing indolent or ignoble, then take heart and march on; but those who have not so trained may leave and go where they will.[5]

And then they set off. The judges and other officials led the way; then came the athletes (numbering perhaps as many as 200) and their entourages, who were followed in their turn by the horses and chariots, along with their owners and riders, and then by the inevitable hangers-on. The Sacred Way on which they walked meandered down the northwest coast of the Peloponnese before turning inland; on the way, as was typical for Greek processions, they stopped from time to time at significant places to perform a sacrifice or carry out some other rite. The first day's journey brought them within striking distance of Olympia. They spent the night out in the open under the growing moon and continued on their way towards the Altis at daybreak.

It might seem strange to subject the contestants to a long walk in the heat, and then an uncomfortable night outdoors, immediately before they were due to compete, but again we need to remember that the ritual aspects of the festival were as important as the games themselves. Besides, all the contestants were equal in this respect – they all suffered the same disadvantage; and the aim at all the ancient Greek games was not for the athletes to break records but to defeat their opponents. So if everyone started equal, no one could complain.

When they reached Olympia in the early afternoon, they were greeted by priests, who came and purified them with water and pig's blood (a familiar purifying agent in Greek religion). Then they made a grand entry into the Altis, to the applause of the spectators who had emerged from their tent city. The athletes' first duty was to accompany the judges to the council house to sacrifice a boar. It was here that competitors were assigned to age classes, but first both the athletes and the judges swore their solemn oaths over slices of boar's flesh before a statue of Zeus *Horkios* – Zeus the god of oaths. In each hand the grim statue held a thunderbolt to strike down those who betrayed their oath. In a paperless society, oaths had to be taken seriously.

Contests took place on this first day (or at least they did from 396 BCE onwards), but they did not involve the athletes, who were allowed to rest after their long walk. These first contests involved trumpeters and town criers (or heralds), and they were as keenly contested as the athletic events. The contestants stood on a platform, so that they could be seen and heard. The winners of the two matches became the official public address system for the duration of the games. It was the trumpeter's job to signal the last lap of the horse races, but his main task was to call for silence whenever it was time for an announcement, and then the town crier's great voice delivered the news – perhaps announcing the next event and summoning the contestants for it, or proclaiming the official winner of an event. When Nero hijacked the games in 67 CE, he made sure that he won the town-crier competition as well, so that he could announce his own further victories. Visiting diplomats might use the town crier to promulgate important political news. As the contestants entered the stadium or the hippodrome one by one, the crier called out their names and the states they represented. This was an opportunity for fans from across Greece to express noisy support for their local heroes; members of the public might also raise objections to certain contestants, claiming that they were not in fact Greek, or were not of good standing in their community.

THE ATHLETIC PROGRAMME

The athletic contests began on the second day. For all the great fame of the games, it is very difficult to reconstruct the programme in all its details, not least because they probably changed over the course of time. Moreover, the judges had the right to change the sequence of events if there were good reasons for doing so. The table below is no more than a likely scenario of the sequence of events in, say, the middle of the fourth century BCE, based on the assumption that it was then a five-day festival

THE ORDER OF EVENTS

Day 1   Procession into Altis; classification of athletes and horses; swearing of oaths; town criers and trumpeters.

Day 2   Many sacrifices; equestrian events; pentathlon; evening sacrifice of a black ram to Pelops.

Night of days 2–3   Full moon.

Day 3   Foot races; the great procession, hecatomb and feast.

Day 4   Combat events; race in armour; boys' events.*

Day 5   Crowning of victors in temple of Zeus; banquet for the victors.

* These may have been movable, or not run all on the same day.

The ancient Olympics featured far fewer events than their modern counterpart – no synchronized swimming or beach volleyball – in fact, there were no team sports at all, because individual achievement was what mattered. Nor, despite the Greekness of their names, were there gymnastic competitions or a marathon race.* The Greeks engaged in ball games, pole vaulting (over a horse, and probably for distance rather than height), swimming for sport, weightlifting and boating, but these activities never became events at the Olympics or any of the major games. One or two new events were introduced, only to be dropped sooner or later. In the third century BCE, the addition of certain events led to the games stretching over six days, rather than the traditional five.

DATES OF INTRODUCTION OF EVENTS TO THE GAMES [6]

EVENT	INTRODUCED	OLYMPIAD
c.200 m sprint (*stadion*)	776	1
c.400 m run (*diaulos*)	724	14
distance run (*dolikhos*)	720	15
pentathlon	708	18
wrestling (*palē*)	708	18
boxing (*pyx*)	688	23
four-horse chariot race (*tethrippon*)	680	25
all-in wrestling (*pankration*)	648	33
horse race (*kelēs*)	648	33
boys' *stadion*	632	37
boys' wrestling	632	37
boys' pentathlon*	628	38
boys' boxing	616	41
c.400 m run in armour (*hoplitodromos*)	520	65
mule-cart race (*apēnē*)**	500	70
horse race for mares (*kalpē*)**	496	71
two-horse chariot race (*synoris*)	408	93
town criers and trumpeters	396	96
four-colt chariot race	384	99
two-colt chariot race	264	129
horse race for colts	256	131
boys' *pankration*	200	145

* *Dropped immediately*
** *Dropped in 444*

---

*   See the appendix on the marathon.

HAIL TO THE VICTOR!

On the fifth and final day, after all the competitions had taken place, the victors made their way to the temple of Zeus. On their heads were tied the fillets or ribbons with which they had been presented immediately after being proclaimed victors in their respective events, and in their hands were palm fronds. This was the day of the formal prize-giving. As they paraded towards the temple, flowers and fruit were tossed in their way, as tokens of the good things they had in store, blessed as they were by the gods. A hymn was sung, including the repeated refrain *tēnella kallinike*, 'hail to the victor!' The victors were then called up one by one by the town crier, who proclaimed each of them 'the best of the Greeks' in his discipline. The wreaths had been laid on a gold and ivory table, and as they went up they were each handed one, which they tied on to their own heads, before making their way to the victors' banquet. With both fillet and wreath, they resembled the figure of Victory that Pheidias' Zeus held in his outstretched right hand.

On returning to his home town, a victor could expect further – and sometimes extravagant – celebrations. When Exaenetus of Acragas in Sicily (modern Agrigento) won the stade race in 412 for the second time in succession, he was escorted back into his home town by 300 chariots drawn by white horses, and a section of the city wall was breached to let him in – the message being that the city had no need of defensive walls when it had a hero of the stature of Exaenetus.[7]

After the games, an Olympic victor might also contemplate dedicating an offering in the Altis, perhaps a statue or a weapon (as a symbol of victory). One athlete, the sprinter Eubatus of Cyrene, was so confident of victory in 408 that he brought a ready-made statue with him, for immediate dedication; he did indeed win. Such a dedication was a thanks offering to the gods. The museum at Olympia remains full of such treasures: a copy of a statue of the god Hermes by Praxiteles of Athens, the most famous sculptor of his day (the mid-fourth century), the original having been stolen by the Romans at some point; a striking terracotta statue of Zeus and his young beloved Ganymede, still with plenty of the original paint in place; the remains of Paeonius of Mende's Victory; marvellous painted pottery; intricately wrought gold diadems; countless bronze artefacts, great and small – tripods, cauldrons, decorated shields, and even the helmet dedicated by Miltiades of Athens after his world-changing victory over the Persians at Marathon in 490 BCE. It is not just the quantity of the pieces, but their quality that stands out. The Olympic festival endured for approximately 1,100 years, and it was always a place of dedication. A tour of the modern museum truly gives one a sense of the splendour that was Olympia, and of the pride that made it so.

After the miraculous defeat of the Persians by the Athenians at Marathon in 490 BCE, the victorious Athenian general, Miltiades, dedicated his helmet at Olympia.

The events

The Greeks divided their athletic events into two main categories. There were the 'gymnic' events, for which the contestants were naked, and the 'hippic' or equestrian events, the horse races and chariot races. The gymnic disciplines were further subdivided. The 'heavy' events were those in which, since there were no weight classes in ancient Greek athletics, heavier contestants tended to have an advantage: wrestling, boxing and pankration. The 'light' events, which we would call track-and-field events, were the running races, long jump, javelin and discus.

The most prestigious events were the four-horse chariot race, which was the first athletic contest at every Olympics, and the stade sprint, which was believed to have been the original event of the earliest games. As noted earlier, it became the custom to name the entire Olympiad after the winner of the sprint. This event was valued much as the 100 metres is today, as a swift expression of stamina, skill and willpower. The four-horse chariot race was the event the spectators found most exciting to watch, for much the same reason that Formula One racing is popular today – that is, the pleasure of watching very expensive vehicles driven with consummate skill under extremely dangerous conditions.

THE EQUESTRIAN EVENTS

On the second day, following a procession by the athletes and Olympic officials around the many altars of the Altis, the athletic programme kicked off with the equestrian events. They probably started early in the morning, because there were several events and they must have taken some time to organize and complete. The hippodrome at Olympia lay to the south of the stadium, between the stadium and the River Alpheus. It was probably laid out at the same time as the new stadium in the middle of the

This black-figure vase from late-sixth-century Athens shows horses rounding the turning post in a race.

fourth century BCE. It consisted of a great expanse of level ground, with little equipment apart from a starting mechanism set back from the western end of the track and an ornate turning post at either end of the course. The post at the western end also marked the end of a lap and therefore the finish. There were presumably barriers between the spectators and the track.

The area of the hippodrome still awaits excavation, but we know that there was space for up to forty chariots to compete. The track seems to have been about 600 metres (660 yards) long and at least 200 metres (220 yards) wide; there were two separate straights, joined by a semicircular arc at either end where the chariots or horses made their turns. A full lap would therefore be about 1,200 metres, almost three-quarters of a mile. The track must have been divided down the middle, perhaps just by a length of uncut grass and weeds between the turning posts (not by anything more solid, because we hear of head-on collisions when chariots veered across the central divide).

The starting gates or stalls were set back from the track, and were ingeniously designed to release the chariots or horses onto the track in an equitable fashion. The device was triangular in shape, with the apex of the triangle pointing towards the track. The starting gates stretched back one by one from the apex, down the sides of the triangle, which were more than 120 metres (130 yards) long. Each starting gate was closed by a length of rope that ran along the sides of the triangle. When the mechanism was released, the ropes of the two gates furthest back from the apex dropped to the ground, releasing the horses. By the time these two horses or chariots reached the position of the next gates forward, the next two stretches of rope had dropped, and so on until all the contestants reached the front at the same time, and thundered up to the starting line. It takes a few sentences to describe, but it all happened very fast. Plainly, the horses at the back had an advantage, in that they would be moving faster by the time they reached the starting line than those further forward, but this compensated them proportionately for the distance they were from the favourable centre of the track. Starting gates were assigned by lot.

The first event to be run was the four-horse chariot race, the most aristocratic of the events; it was run over twelve laps – somewhat more than 8 miles (13 km) – so it was a long and arduous event. This was followed by the horse race (a flat race, we would call it) over two laps, then the two-horse chariot race over eight laps, and the four-colt chariot race, also over eight laps. In the middle of the fourth century, that was all, as far as equestrian events were concerned. As we have seen, two more equestrian events were added to the programme temporarily in the fifth century, and another two, a two colt chariot race and a regular flat race for colts, were added in the third century. Horses and colts might be either male or female; they were unshod.

In the days before stirrups and saddles,* horseback riding was far more uncomfortable and dangerous than it is today. They had bridles and bits, of course, because without them horses are unmanageable, and jockeys carried switches. The highly trained, expert riders were young, slightly built slaves, and it was not uncommon for them to fall off. The horses used by the Greeks seem to have been somewhat smaller than ours nowadays, but it would still be a hard fall and, even apart from broken bones, fatalities were not unknown.

It is curious that, although most of the Olympic events were about the expenditure of individual effort, the owners of the horses that took part in the equestrian events got the credit for victory (or the shame of loss) even though they had probably done little more than pay the necessary expenses. In this context, there is a very telling story. In 512, one jockey fell off right at the

---

* Stirrup-less saddles may have been introduced in the first century BCE.

start of the race, but the well-trained riderless horse continued and even put on a spurt when it heard the signal for the final lap. It came first – and its owner was awarded first prize.[1] The horse, apparently, was the equivalent of a human athlete; the slave jockey, for all his skill, was considered, in this case at least, no more than a steering mechanism.

Mere ownership of horses eventually allowed even women to gain the glory of Olympic victory. In 396, Agesilaus II of Sparta encouraged his sister Cynisca to enter a four-horse chariot. He was annoyed by people bragging of their victories in the event, and wanted to prove 'that to keep such a team was not a mark of manly virtue, but only of wealth'.[2] Cynisca was unable to be there to see it happen, but her chariot won. The inscribed base of the statue group she set up has survived, and it shows that, despite her brother's manipulation, she was proud of her victory: 'I declare myself the only woman in all Greece to have won this crown.'[3] In later years, however, other women repeated Cynisca's feat – always in the equestrian events, naturally. We know of three other female Olympic winners, with four further victories between them.* But the feat remained rare, because in most Greek states women were not allowed to own property such as horses.

A racing chariot was simple and light – not much more than a wooden platform on two four-spoked wheels, with a wicker superstructure – and it lacked suspension, so that it must have been a rough ride. On a four-horse chariot, the horses were abreast of one another, with the two inner horses joined to the yoke, and the two outer horses harnessed only by traces (leather straps running horizontally down the horse's side). As well as

---

* Cynisca won in 396 and again in 392; the other women were Euryleonis of Sparta (winner of the two-horse chariot race a few decades after Cynisca), Bilstiche of Macedon (winner of the four-colt chariot race in 268 and the two-colt race in 264), and Theodota of Elis in the first century BCE, winning the two-colt race. Other women were victors at other festivals, but these are all we know from the Olympics.

reins, the charioteer wielded a whip. Chariot races were extremely dangerous; crashes, especially as the chariots rounded the turn, were frequent. At the turn, the chariots bunched up, because to take the turn too wide would be a sure way to fall behind, and it was all too easy for wheels to clash with wheels. Again, fatalities were not uncommon. In 462, at the Pythian games, only one out of forty chariots completed the race; in 416, only four of Alcibiades' seven chariots finished the course at Olympia (see p. 67).

The Athenian dramatist Sophocles included a vivid, brutal description of a chariot race in his play *Electra*, written around 415 BCE. It really makes the event come alive. An old retainer of Orestes is trying to convince someone that his master died during the Pythian games at Delphi:

> But when one of the gods is against you, not even the strong can escape. When the day of the swift chariot race dawned, he entered the contest along with many other charioteers... Their starting positions were decided by lot, and the appointed judges put them in their places, until at the sound of the bronze trumpet off they raced, calling out to their horses and shaking the reins with their hands. The whole course was filled with the rattle of chariots; dust rose into the air; they were all tightly bunched together... So far all the chariots had remained upright, but as they came out of the turn from the sixth to the seventh lap, the Aenean's hard-mouthed horses lunged abruptly forward and crashed straight into the Barcaean chariot. After that, as a result of this single accident, one collided and smashed into another, until the whole track was filled with wrecked chariots. When he realized what was going on, the Athenian charioteer cleverly pulled his team aside and reined them in, so as to pass the seething chaos of the surging mass of horses in the middle of the track. Orestes was in the rear, holding his horses back and trusting that the final stretch would bring him victory. When he saw that there was only one other contestant left, he hurled a shrill command into the ears of his swift horses and set off after him. The two teams were neck and neck, with first one and then the other a head in front of his rival.

Orestes kept the hub of his left wheel close to the post at every turn and gave the right-hand trace-horse its head. He succeeded in keeping the nearest wheel away from the post on every turn, and the poor man remained safely standing, with his chariot upright, for all the remaining laps, until on the final lap he slackened the left rein before the horse had made the turn and grazed the edge of the post. The hub of the wheel split and he was hurled over the chariot's rail. He became tangled in the reins, and as he fell to the ground his horses were scattered all over the track.

At the sight of his fall from the chariot, the crowd cried out in grief that the young man should meet with such misfortune after having achieved so much. At one time he was dashed to the ground, at another his feet were tossed skyward, until the other charioteers were finally able to check his horses' rush and free his blood-streaked body. Not even any of his friends would have recognized the wretched corpse.[4]

THE PENTATHLON

The next event, occupying the afternoon of the second day, was the pentathlon, the 'five-fold contest'. The order in which the five events were contested was probably discus, jump, javelin, sprint and wrestling (saving the toughest for last). Since it combined both heavy and light disciplines, the pentathlon was commonly held to be the best all-round test of physical fitness, and was praised as such by philosophers as well as physicians. Aristotle, for instance, said: 'For a young man, beauty is having a body that is apt for the exertions involved in foot races and feats of strength, while he himself is pleasing for others to look upon and enjoy; this is why pentathletes are especially beautiful, because they are naturally suited for both strength and speed.'[5] The first three events – discus, jump and javelin – were peculiar to the pentathlon and were never independent events at Olympia.

Discuses were originally made of stone, but later bronze or iron. The most common weight was about 2 kilograms (4.5 lbs; the same as the modern discus), but there are extant examples from under 1.5 kilograms (3.3 lbs) to over 4.5 kilograms (10 lbs). One theory is that a contestant might choose a heavier discus as a challenge to the rest, who were obliged to match his weight; it is more likely, however, that the heavier discuses were just impressive dedications for the sanctuary, not for actual use. The discus was thrown with feet planted and a twist of the body, but not with the full-bodied spin that athletes employ nowadays. The results were therefore disappointing by today's standards.

Javelins were about 2 metres (6.5 ft) long. They were made of elder wood, with metal points, and each of them had a leather thong wrapped around the shaft which acted as a kind of sling as the javelin was released and imparted a rotary motion to it which stabilized its flight. Modern experiments have shown that throwers can gain quite a bit of extra length thanks to the thong. These javelins were specifically designed for sport; they were lighter than military javelins and bore a less lethal head. The athlete ran up and released the javelin, aiming to throw it as far as he could, not to hit a target. Judging by what we see in pictorial media, the athlete tried to get extra power into his throw by turning the upper part of his body back along the line of the javelin before twisting around and releasing it.

The nature of the jump is made controversial by ancient claims that on two occasions athletes jumped over 50 feet (15–16 metres).[6] Either we have to reject this evidence and assume that the jump was a single jump, like our long jump, or we can accept it and say that the jump was a triple jump (sometimes referred to as the hop, step and jump). There are other possibilities, such as a series of standing jumps, but scholars are pretty evenly divided between the first two. There was a take-off board, and

a clean landing with clear footprints in the sand was required for the jump to be valid. The jumpers were accompanied by the music of a reed pipe (an *aulos*, with a sound rather like an oboe), which was supposed to help their rhythm. The role of piper was assigned to whomever had won the *aulos* contest at the Pythia in Delphi two years previously. A jumper also carried hand weights of 1–2 kilograms (2–4.5 lbs), which were supposed to help him gain distance by gaining height, if he swung them forward and up as he took off, and then swung his arms behind him, and perhaps dropped them behind him, as he began to land. Modern experiments have been inconclusive.

The rules governing the pentathlon are obscure, and all solutions are controversial. How many throws of the discus and javelin was each contestant allowed? How many jumps? Above all, how was the winner chosen? They did not have a points system of the kind we use for the present-day decathlon and heptathlon, for which accurate measurements are needed. We know that the first three events formed a distinct triad, so it seems likely that the judges employed a knockout system. In the preliminary training in Elis, it would be easy for them to reduce the field to sixteen or some other convenient number. Then each athlete contested the first triad of events with the opponent against whom he was drawn, and so on up to and including the quarter-final round; the run was reserved for the semi-finals, and the wrestling for the finals.

RUNNING

'Victory by speed of foot is honoured above all,' sang Xenophanes of Colophon – before launching into his iconoclastic diatribe against athletics (see p. 66). The morning of the third, central day

A copy of the famous 'Discus-thrower' by Myron (mid-fifth century), brilliantly showing the energy and action of the athlete.

of the Olympic festival was devoted to the three foot races. The judges entered the stadium first and took their seats, while the athletes waited in the vaulted entrance tunnel until their names were called. One by one, they disrobed and ran out into the sunshine to the roars of the crowd. Their lanes had been assigned by lot. There might be as many as twenty starters in each race, and once in a while a single athlete won all three and was hailed as a triple winner. Incredibly, Leonidas of Rhodes was a triple winner at four successive Olympics between 164 and 152. The fact that all three races were held on the same day makes this rare achievement all the more remarkable, and heats may have been run as well.

They ran in bare feet, of course, and stood upright at the starting line (a stone sill with grooves for the toes), waiting for the knee-high rope that was stretched across their fronts to drop, signalling the start of the race. As today's runners do, while waiting for the start the contestants kept their muscles warm with light exercises and stretches. The starting commands were 'Foot by foot!' (that is, place your feet on the starting grooves) and then 'Go!' – *poda para poda... apite.*

The *dolikhos*, the 'long run', was the first event – twelve laps or twenty-four lengths of the stadium at Olympia (fewer elsewhere), with all the runners turning anticlockwise around a single central post. The turn was tight, and runners were not allowed to use their hands to slingshot around the post. Each lap was not far short of 400 metres, so the *dolikhos* distance was almost three miles. Then it was the sprint – the stade race, one length of the stadium, which at Olympia was about 192 metres (210 yards). For this race, the runners started at the eastern end of the stadium, so that they could finish at the western end, close to the Altis and Zeus' altar, as was traditional. The sprint was followed by the *diaulos*, the 'double pipe', two lengths of the stadium; runners occupied alternate lanes for this event, since each runner turned at his

This black-figure vase, attributed to the Euphiletos painter (*c.* 530 BCE), shows sprinters: note the bulging thighs and urgent forward posture.

own post (anticlockwise, as usual) and ran back along the other lane. Victors were immediately announced by the town crier, and victory laps of the stadium to receive the applause of the crowd were as common then as today.

THE HEAVY EVENTS

The rest of the third day was given over to the hecatomb sacrifice and then to feasting. On the morning of the fourth day, the heavy events took place in the stadium; wrestling and pankration on a patch of ground where the earth had been dug up and loosened and then covered in sand, and boxing on some level ground. The lack of weight categories favoured heavier fighters. Opponents were determined by drawing lots, and lots were drawn for every round of the competitions, which were organized as knockouts. The fighters were required to sprinkle dust on themselves to allow their opponents to get a grip on their oiled bodies – though we hear of unscrupulous wrestlers using their oily hands to wipe the dust off a part of the body that was likely to be targeted by an opponent.

There were no timed rounds in any of the heavy events, so contestants required stamina as well as skill, but presumably their contests were shorter than ours, since they would soon suffer from exhaustion. Even so, the heavy events were so demanding that it added to the lustre of victory in any of them if the victor fought every round, without having received a bye. It is clear from the various descriptions of these events that their attraction (if that is the right word) was the same then as now – a combination of admiring strength and skill, and waiting for the blood to spurt.

These were violent sports, and would certainly be banned or toned down nowadays, but ancient Greek attitudes towards

The starting-line. Before a race, runners adopted an upright posture with their toes in the grooves, waiting for the signal to begin.

violence and death were different from ours – more callous or more matter-of-fact, depending on one's point of view – and both injury and death were regarded as things to be endured or even sought in the pursuit of glory. Deaths in the Olympic heavy events were rare, but common enough for provisions to be in place exempting a contestant from legal charges if he killed his opponent during a festival. Nor was killing an opponent a reason for denying a contestant victory, unless the lethal blow was illegal. Of the six or so sports-related deaths that we know of, all but one occurred at Olympia. Heat exhaustion, as well as physical injury, may well have been a factor. One pankratiast, Arrachion of Phigaleia, died – probably of sudden heart failure, a not unknown cause of death for athletes nowadays either – at the moment of defeating his opponent; his corpse was duly crowned with the victory olive wreath.[7]

In boxing, any form of blow was allowed, provided it landed on the head or neck; body blows were either not allowed or were considered unsportsmanlike, and clinching, the bane of modern boxing, was forbidden also. The boxers wore no padded gloves (except in training), but light, criss-crossed leather straps (*himantes*) on their hands for protection: 'The four fingers were bound up so that they extended beyond the strap sufficiently to allow the boxer to clench his fist,' wrote Philostratus in the third century CE; in other words, the straps formed a boxer's hand into a kind of club.[8] The slang name for the *himantes* was *myrmikes* ('ants'), because they stung and nicked the face. Thus equipped, they battered each other until one was compelled to admit defeat – the loser signalled submission with a hand gesture – or was incapable of continuing. It was not up to the judges to bring a fight to an end, even if one man was obviously in trouble. If a bout was going on too long, the judges ordered the enfeebled combatants to exchange blows, even blows to the body, without defending themselves, until they had a result.

There was no roped-off boxing ring as such, but the fighters were hemmed in by spectators, and the referees made sure that they remained within striking distance of each other. In the fourth century, a hardened leather knucklepad was introduced, which had two consequences: injuries became more severe, and a more defensive form of boxing became dominant. Melancomas of Caria was said to be able to keep his guard up for two whole days, so that despite his long career his face remained unscarred.[9] He defeated his opponents while hardly striking or taking a blow, but just by skipping around them ('floating like a butterfly', perhaps, as Muhammad Ali was famously to put it), defending against their blows, and waiting for them to be too tired to carry on. Otherwise, the ancient Greeks apparently enjoyed seeing two men beat each other's faces to a bloody pulp. You could usually tell a boxer by his scarred face and cauliflower ears. One epitaph for a boxer who died at Olympia says simply: 'He prayed to Zeus for the crown or for death.'[10] A boxer called Eurydamas, from Cyrene in North Africa, was hit so hard in the face that several of his teeth came loose; judging that if he spat them out his opponent would see that he was in trouble, he swallowed them.[11]

The brutality of ancient Greek boxing comes alive in a passage from a poem by Theocritus, writing in the third century BCE, in which a son of Zeus, Polydeuces (one of the 'Heavenly Twins', usually called Castor and Pollux in English), is pitted against Amycus, a gigantic, brutish son of the god Poseidon.[12] First, the two opponents circle each other, manoeuvring so as to get the sun shining in the other's eyes. Our hero, Polydeuces, lands the first blow on his opponent's chin, which enrages Amycus, who begins to swing wildly.

> Then the son of Zeus, shifting this way and that, cut him with
> both hands, one after the other, and checked the onslaught of
> the son of Poseidon, for all his overwhelming strength. He
> stood there, drunk from the blows, spitting red blood... and as

his face swelled, his eyes began to close. Polydeuces set out to confuse his opponent by feinting from all directions, and when he saw that he was at his mercy, he drove his fist into his brow, above the nose, and opened up his forehead to the bone, stretching Amycus out on his back among the flowers.

The contest became ferocious when Amycus regained his feet. Lashing out with their hard leather gloves, it turned into a fight to the death. Amycus aimed at Polydeuces' chest and body, but the invincible Polydeuces kept pummelling his opponent's face with disfiguring blows... And then Amycus, looking for a breakthrough, grasped Polydeuces' left hand in his, leaned forward and to the other side, and swung his great fist up from the level of his right hip. If the blow had landed, it would have done Polydeuces serious injury, but he ducked and at the same time landed a mighty blow under Amycus' left temple, with his arm at full stretch from his shoulder. Immediately, dark blood gushed from the gaping wound on Amycus' temple. Polydeuces followed this with a left to the mouth, loosening the giant's teeth. Faster and faster he rained punishing blows on Amycus' face, smashing his cheeks to pulp. And Amycus lay stretched out on the ground, dazed, and held up both hands in surrender, since he was close to death.

Wrestling was again somewhat different from the modern event. Wrestlers grappled upright, with no part of the body except the feet allowed on the ground. In the starting position, the wrestlers leaned forward with their foreheads touching (butting like rams, as the Greeks put it) and grasped each other's hand, wrist or forearm; the bout began with them circling around, looking for an advantage. A win was gained by three throws (a contest therefore involved a maximum of five bouts) – by some part of the loser's back, shoulders, chest or stomach having touched the ground, in the opinion of the judges, three times. It was acceptable for a knee to touch the ground, because certain throws used the knee as a pivot. There was no need to pin an opponent down for a count; even grazing the ground would be enough. The judges looked for evidence in the form of sand stuck to the faller's skin.

Essentially, wrestling was a contest of skill and technique, but all kinds of tactics were permitted, including strangleholds, tripping, leg tackles and bending back fingers. Breaking fingers appears to have been illegal, though we are told that a wrestler called Leontiscus of Messana (in Sicily) won by this method in the middle of the fifth century. After that, the practice was, in theory, banned.[13] Cleitostratus of Rhodes was known for weakening his opponents with a chokehold and then throwing them to the ground. Just as a runner could increase his fame by being a triple winner, so it was considered especially glorious for a wrestler to have won without having been thrown, let alone without having been awarded a bye. The enormous popularity of wrestling is shown not just by the presence in every Greek town of any size of at least one palaestra (wrestling club), but also by the frequency with which it occurs as a metaphor in all kinds of ancient literature. A 'third fall', for instance, was a common way of saying 'defeat'.

Pankration was unique, in the ancient world, to the Greeks and Romans; it resembled the sport today called 'mixed martial arts' – or sometimes the 'modern pankration'. The Greek word means 'total force', and a pankration bout could turn extremely nasty. The point was to inflict so much pain on your opponent that he gave up and signalled his submission. Punching and kicking were the basic techniques, and fighters sometimes wore protective straps like boxers, but the contestants often fell to grappling on the ground. In theory, biting, gouging and kneeing the genitals were forbidden, but fighters occasionally seem to have been able to get away with these tactics. They were certainly allowed to butt an opponent with their heads and stamp on him when he was on the ground. 'A pankratiast', as Pindar put it, 'must use all possible means to eliminate his rival.'[14] Vase paintings

overleaf
Wrestlers in the starting position at the beginning
of a bout. The Greeks called the position the 'ram'.

depict men with bloody handprints on their bodies, and we hear of a wide variety of horrible injuries. Pankration was not for the faint-hearted, and at least one athlete, Sarapion of Alexandria, is known to have withdrawn from the contest when he saw the size of his opponent.[15] This had happened at other games, but it was the only time it had ever happened at the Olympics, and he was duly fined for cowardice.

THE RACE IN ARMOUR

The fourth day of the festival was the final day of competition. It ended with the gruelling race in armour and then (following the order of events presented in the previous chapter) the boys' events.* The race in armour, the *hoplitodromos*, was run over the length of the stadium and back again (like the *diaulos*), a distance

---

* I will say nothing about the boys' events – the sprint, wrestling and boxing – because they were simply junior versions of what I have already described.

of about a quarter of a mile (400 m). That was a moderate distance compared with the equivalent race at other venues, which could be as long as 2 miles (3 km). Contestants originally wore a crested bronze helmet on their head and bronze greaves on their shins, and carried a hoplite shield, which was a large and awkward object, and it was not unknown for athletes to fumble it during the race. Armour was notoriously ill-fitting as well, to add to their discomfort.

Hoplites were the heavy infantry of Greek armies. The shield was about a metre (3 ft) in diameter (more than half a man's height), concave, and consisted of a thin layer of bronze on a wooden frame, with leather padding and hand grips inside, and a protective bronze band all the way around the rim. The weight of shields for military use varied between 6 and 8 kilograms (13–17 lb), so at Olympia the runners carried specially made shields which were all of the same weight. In Pausanias' day in the second century CE, twenty-five of these shields were stored on the site, in the temple of Zeus.[16] And by Pausanias' time the contestants were required to carry only the shield; the helmet and greaves had been dropped.

GAMES FOR GIRLS

Married women were not allowed to attend the Olympics, but unmarried women were, and so was the local priestess of Demeter. 'Unmarried women' (*parthenoi* in Greek) actually means young girls, since they were invariably married off by the age of fourteen or fifteen, the idea being to confine their sexuality within the bonds of marriage as soon as possible after puberty. It may seem odd that married rather than young, unmarried women were prevented from seeing naked men, but this is just another

A snapshot from a sixth-century vase of the tough race in armour. Note especially the size and awkwardness of the shields.

occasion when Greek practices confound the modern mind. In any case, the prohibition says more about Greek attitudes to women than it does about any sense of modesty or the opposite.

Female games took place at several locations around the Greek world. At Olympia, they were sacred to Hera, Zeus' wife, rather than Zeus himself, and they were for girls, not women. The occasion of the games was the ritual presentation of Hera's new robe to her cult statue, with dancing, sacrifices and feasting afterwards; this happened once every four years, so there was the same interval between festivals as for the Olympics.

A one-stade sprint seems to have been the only event (as it was at other festivals with events for women), but the stadium was shortened for the girls by one-sixth, to 500 rather than 600 Olympic feet – about 160 metres in our terms. There seems to be no good reason for this other than to assert male superiority.* The girls were divided into three age categories, with the youngest going first, so the whole festival would have been over in a day. The winners received a crown of olive, just as at the male Olympics. Other than this, we know very little about this Heraea festival, and almost everything about it is controversial. Victorious girls were allowed to erect commemorative statues, just as men were, but none of the statues, nor their inscribed pedestals, have survived to help fill in the gaps in our knowledge.

We do not know when the games started, and it is quite possible that they were late additions to the festival calendar of Olympia. Why else would we hear nothing about them until Pausanias wrote about them in the second century CE?[17] We also do not know whether the contestants were only local girls, or came from further afield as well, but the use of the Olympic stadium suggests that the games were international, even if to a lesser degree than the male games. Nor do we even know at what

---

* Like the so-called 'ladies' tees' in golf, a term resented by many.

time of year the Heraea were held, though it is possible that they took place immediately before the male Olympics. This would explain why girls were present as spectators at the main event; they were the competitors left over from the Heraea.

The female games were initiatory in character; as in other Greek rites, running was supposed to 'tame' a girl and prepare her for womanhood and marriage. This raises a curious possibility. Many of the male athletes at the Olympics would have been in their mid-twenties, close to the age of marriage for men, and the girls' fathers or guardians, who would have accompanied and chaperoned their daughters, perhaps took the opportunity to pick out prospective husbands, now that their daughters were close to womanhood. It is conceivable, then, that the homoeroticism of the ancient Olympics was tempered by a little hetero-eroticism.*

It was common in the Archaic and early Classical period for members of the elite to enter into marriage alliances with equivalently high-ranking families from other city states, and the crown games were where the elite met and mingled. When Cleisthenes, the ruler of Sicyon early in the sixth century, wanted to find a husband for his daughter, he made the announcement at Olympia. Any man who thought he had what it took to be his son-in-law should present himself at Sicyon, where he would compete against other suitors in athletic events for a full year before Cleisthenes made his decision. (The eventual winner, Megacles of Athens, was himself an Olympic victor in the four-horse chariot race.) The practice of using Olympia for matchmaking declined in later centuries – Athens, for instance, made it a condition of citizenship in the mid-fifth century that both parents should be Athenian citizens, effectively banning foreign marriages – but still, for some the games may have had this extra social function.

---

* By coincidence, a marriageable girl was the prize of athletic contests in some modern Greek villages as recently as the early twentieth century.

The spectators of the Heraea included men. It is unlikely that the girls ran naked or oiled their bodies. One of the curiosities in the Olympia museum is a miniature bronze group of naked dancing girls, dating from the eighth century, but that may have nothing to do with the Heraea. Girls and women were generally expected to be modest. There was a similar initiatory run for girls at the temple of Artemis in Brauron, a town near Athens, at which the girls wore light dresses which were then shed *after* the run to symbolize their coming of age. This was a run, not a competitive race, but it is likely that at Olympia too the girls wore a knee-length, loose-fitting dress of some kind. According to Pausanias, they ran in a garment that left their right breast and shoulder exposed. This seems odd for an athletic garment. It must have had ritual purposes, and it may have been an imitation of the garb worn by men for strenuous activities such as hunting. That would make sense in the context of an initiatory event, because cross-dressing is a common initiatory practice in cultures all around the world.

There are two pieces in existence, a statue and a statuette, which show young women wearing just such a costume, but it is not clear that they are runners, rather than dancers. Or perhaps they are runners who have turned to dancing? We can date these pieces, or the originals on which they were based, but if they portray dancers rather than runners, they do not help us to date the start of the girls' games at Olympia. If, on the other hand, they do portray runners, then that supports a start date of the Heraea in the sixth century BCE, which is what Pausanias implies. The Heraea remain frustratingly shrouded in darkness, a product of male indifference to the practices of womenfolk.

A statue of a girl wearing the kind of costume that girls might have worn when competing at the Heraea at Olympia.

Heroes and victors

It is time to meet some of the greatest ancient Greek athletes, not just because they are a source of good stories, but for the light they shed on the culture of ancient Greek athletics. The Greeks had no way of keeping records that depended on the accurate measurement of time, but that did not matter to the Olympic contestants. The point was to win on the day – to beat your rivals – and that was all that counted. Nevertheless, the Greeks did keep records in the sense that they remembered particularly spectacular feats, and they were perennially fascinated by who was the first to do something, whether that involved a new discovery, such as how to make wine, or an especially long jump. This was a sure route to celebrity status in ancient Greece. Many surviving Olympic inscriptions boast of such achievements. Muhammad Ali was not the first to come up with the phrase 'I am the greatest'; we have seen something close to the ancient equivalent of his words on Cynisca's inscription, for instance (see p. 110). The Greeks could recognize an outstanding athlete when they saw one and gave him due credit. Quite often, in fact, they gave rather too much credit: these men were popular heroes, and fanciful tales grew up around them.

But the actual athletic achievements of such men were rarely exaggerated, because everyone knew the facts; these men were famous all over the Greek world, so that exaggerations would quickly be exposed for what they were. The memory of past achievements, as relayed in popular tales or inscribed on statue pedestals, acted as a spur to ambitious athletes. Pantacles of Athens was the first runner to win in successive Olympics (in 696 and 692). The first to beat Pantacles' achievement was Chionis of Sparta, who won both the *stadion* and the *diaulos* at a single Olympics, and went on to do so at three successive Olympics between 664 and 656. That remarkable record stood for a long time, but in 520 another short race was added to the Olympic programme, the race in armour (*hoplitodromos*), and that made it possible for a single athlete to win all three short races in a single Olympics. Phanas of Pellene was remembered as the first to have done this, in 512. Then, early in the fifth century a runner called Astylus, who in his time represented both Croton, in southern Italy, and Syracuse in Sicily, equalled the achievements of both Chionis and Phanas.* Again, Astylus' record stood for a long time – it seemed to be unassailable – until in four successive Olympics between 164 and 152 Leonidas of Rhodes – gifted, it was said, with the speed of a god – won all three races. His record remained unbeaten for the rest of Olympic history: Leonidas really was the greatest.

The natural fascination with 'firsts' comes across brilliantly in a first-century CE inscription from the city of Miletus, on the stretch of the west coast of Asia Minor (modern Turkey) known in ancient times as Ionia. The runner – we do not know his name, because the stone is damaged – knew how to advertise his prowess in a way that was sure to catch people's attention. He certainly did not downplay his victories at major games such as the Olympics, but he was particularly concerned to point out when he had been the first to do something. Not only was he the first triple winner at the Nemean games and at the Actia, but he also bundled together as many as possible of his other victories as 'firsts' by gradually narrowing down the geographical scope: for some achievements, he was 'the first man in Asia Minor'; for others only 'the first of the Ionians'; and for yet others 'the first

---

* Interestingly, it was at this point, after Astylus' feat, that the Spartans, Chionis' fellow citizens, erected or re-erected his statue at Olympia, decades after his victories. They made sure that it stood close to that of Astylus, as though to remind Astylus that Chionis had been first, and they also added a few words to the inscription beside his statue – 'There was no *hoplitodromos* at the time' – as though to say that Chionis would have done as well as Astylus if he had had the opportunity. This is a good example of the use of statues for claiming superiority, further discussed in Chapter 7.

from Miletus.'[1] The pride is palpable. Even in the first century CE, the old Homeric sentiment was alive and well – not just to strive always to be the best, superior to all others, but to make sure that others knew it as well.

HEROES

One of the ways in which the Greeks memorialized their athletic heroes is bound to seem very strange to modern minds. Greek religion recognized an intermediate level of supernatural entity between fully fledged gods and mortal human beings. These entities less than gods but more than human – were called 'heroes'. They were people who during their lifetimes had displayed such power that after their deaths they received worship, in order to harness or turn aside that power. The most common fields in which men became heroes were warfare, athletics and city foundation. If a man achieved outstanding success in these activities, it was believed that he must have found favour with the gods, or even that he had been possessed by the relevant god in order to be successful. You wanted such a man on your side, so you gave him honour.

An inscription has survived from the island of Thasos, showing that their most famous athlete, a boxer named Theogenes, winner in over 1,000 contests, was worshipped after his death as a healing hero. Each person sacrificing or praying to him was obliged to pay at least one obol,* and when the total had reached 1,000 drachmas (6,000 sacrifices, if everyone paid the minimum rate) a decision was to be made as to how to spend it on a suitable offering to Theogenes – a statue, perhaps, or a beautifully inscribed epigram by a famous poet.

---

* A Greek coin worth one sixth of a drachma.

A good depiction of the final stance, just before release, of a javelin-thrower, on a fifth-century red-figure vase from Athens.

How did an athlete, even a brilliant one, come to be semi-divine? Although Theogenes died in the fifth century, it was some time before his worship was instituted. Not long after his death, the statue of him that the Thasians had erected in commemoration of his astonishing athletic career fell over and crushed a man – a political enemy of Theogenes who was abusing the statue. Normal Greek practice in such cases was to punish the statue, so they threw it in the sea. However, an indeterminate number of years later Thasos suffered prolonged crop failure; the citizens asked the Delphic oracle what they should do, and were told that they had been neglecting Theogenes and should worship him as a hero. His statue was fortuitously recovered from the sea by a fisherman, his worship was instituted, and the Thasian harvests improved.[2] The base of his statue, which was set up in a central location in the town, has survived.

This story follows a pattern common for heroized athletes. Oebatas of Dyme in Achaea won the stade race in 756, but the Achaeans failed to honour him for his victory, so he cursed them and from then on no Achaean won any victories at Olympia – until they set up a statue for him in Delphi. Euthycles of Locri in southern Italy had been honoured by commemorative statues in his home town, but later he was accused of wrongdoing and the statues were defaced. Famine followed – until they instituted the worship of Euthycles as a hero.

The stories show that it took special circumstances to convert a mortal athletic victor into a hero; it was a rare, not a regular occurrence. The first prerequisite of heroization was that the citizens of the athlete's home town had to remember him, even possibly over many decades, as someone who had achieved greatness, but the second was more random – the occurrence of a chance event that could be directly or indirectly attributed to the man they remembered. In the case of a fellow citizen of Euthycles called Euthymus, it took a simultaneous lightning strike on two of his statues, one in Locri itself and one in Olympia.

With Euthymus, we certainly enter the realm of fable. The town of Temesa (or Tempsa) on the Tyrrhenian Sea was being plagued by the ghost of one of the companions of Odysseus. The story went that when Odysseus' ship called in at Temesa on his way back from the legendary Trojan War, one of his crew tried to rape a local girl, and was stoned to death by the Temesans. Centuries later (the Greeks dated the Trojan War to the twelfth century), the citizens of Temesa began mysteriously dying; so many of them died, in fact, that the survivors were close to abandoning the town. They were told by the Delphic oracle that they had to appease the ghost by giving it, every year, a young woman, a virgin, to be its wife. Euthymus happened to arrive in Temesa just as the first of these sacrifices was about to take place; he was on his way back from Olympia in 472, where he had just won

his third victory in the boxing. He fell in love with the girl, fought and defeated the ghost (which jumped into the sea), and lived happily ever after with his rescued bride. Even Euthymus' death was miraculous: he was simply removed from human sight by

A detail of one of the most famous athletic statues
from the ancient world, *The Boxer at Rest* was discovered
in Rome in 1885. See next page.

the river god he claimed as a father. With such a background, he was obviously a suitable candidate for heroization, but, again, this does not seem to have happened straight away. It took the lightning strikes for the Locrians to see the light.[3]

THEOGENES AND POLYDAMAS

Many of the most famous athletes who participated in the heavy events were, appropriately enough, of very considerable size. Theogenes, who specialized in boxing and pankration, was remembered for his monstrous proportions: it was said that he was a son of Heracles; that he could eat an entire ox at a single sitting and still want more; and that at the age of just eight he had been seen carrying a full-size bronze statue.

A commemorative inscription at Delphi claims that Theogenes won 1,300 victories (and, remarkably, not all in the heavy events), and in Pausanias the number is 1,400. Even if he was not rich before he started, he ended up a multi-millionaire. Among his victories, his feat of winning both the pankration and the boxing at Olympia was especially remembered. 'No mortal had ever achieved that before,' boasted his inscription: we see again the Greek love of 'firsts'.[4] He even named his son Disolympius, 'twice Olympian'. Theogenes' achievement remained unbeaten for almost 280 years, until it was equalled by Cleitomachus of Thebes. Theogenes also won nine times at Nemea, ten times in nine festivals at the Isthmus, and was said to have been undefeated at boxing for twenty-two years. Apart from victories at major international games, the rest of his prizes would have been picked up at local games. He was clearly a professional athlete who spent his time touring the festivals, but at many of the smaller ones it seems unlikely that anyone would have dared to stand up to

The realism of this statue of a boxer, with his
battered face, cauliflower ears and thonged hands,
is typical of the Hellenistic period (323-30).

him. The organizers of the festivals would have been delighted to have him, nevertheless, as his presence was sure to attract a large crowd.

Polydamas of Scotoussa was another whose statue, like that of Theogenes, was credited with healing properties. He was a pankratiast, the winner at Olympia in 408, and the tallest man of his day, according to Pausanias.[5]* Polydamas' feats of strength were legendary: he fought a lion with his bare hands on the slopes of Mount Olympus and won; on another occasion he stopped a fast-moving chariot by seizing hold of it with one hand as it sped past him. Challenged by the king of Persia to take on the strongest of his bodyguards, he fought three of them at once and killed them all. He died in an act of heroic self-sacrifice: when the roof of a cave where he and some friends were drinking began to collapse, Polydamas held it up while the others escaped, at the cost of his own life. In ancient Greece, especially tall men attracted especially tall tales.

This was a society with no newspapers or other reliable sources of information, but people wanted to hear stories of their heroes, and tales such as those about Theogenes and Polydamas fed a public appetite for sensationalism. Athletes in our own day attract hero worship, especially footballers, but pop stars perhaps offer a closer parallel to the kind of adulation that ancient Greek athletes could inspire – and with adulation go far-fetched and fanciful stories. Before we scoff at these ancient tales, we should remember that Elvis Presley's Graceland mansion is a pilgrimage site, and that for many years there was a Church of Elvis in Portland, Oregon. In Jamaica, Bob Marley's status is very close to that of a hero in the ancient Greek sense.

---

*   In the Classical period, the average height for a man was 170 centimetres (5 ft 7 in).

Croton, in southern Italy, was home to a number of outstanding early Olympians. In 576 the first seven finishers in the final of the stade race were all Crotonians – a feat any country today would be more than proud to repeat. At every Olympics between 508 and 480, except one, it was a Crotonian who won the sprint. A proverb was coined: 'The last of the Crotonians is the first of the other Greeks.' Curiously, however, after 480 no Crotonian ever won an Olympic crown in any event. Could this be related to the fact that Croton was inclining towards a more democratic constitution, and perhaps therefore had a lower tolerance of elite pastimes and values? Or could it be that the state had previously sponsored and subsidized athletes, recruiting them even from the lower classes, but after 480 decided to spend its money elsewhere?

The most famous Crotonian of all, and the most famous athlete in the Greek world, was Milo. Milo, it was said, once carried an ox around the stadium at Olympia and then ate it in the course of a single day, and his daily fare consisted of huge amounts of meat, bread and wine. He would stand on a greased discus and challenge men to try to push him off; he would tie a ribbon round his head and burst it by holding his breath and swelling his veins; he could hold a pomegranate in his hand so securely that no one could prise even one finger off the fruit, and yet the fruit remained unmarked and uncrushed. He once saved a group of philosophers when a roof threatened to collapse on them, by replacing the crumbling pillar with his own body until everyone was safe. He was said to have died when he inserted his hands into a cleft in a tree trunk, intending to split it in two; the tree closed on his hands, trapping him, and making him easy prey for a wolf pack.[6]

overleaf
Here we see a trainer about to flog the pankratiasts
for the foul of gouging each other's faces.

Milo was a wrestler. He won at Olympia as a boy, probably in 540, and then another five or six times as an adult. In the tradition that has him winning five adult crowns, he was denied a further win by his canny opponent, another Crotonian, who refused to engage the aged wrestler and let him tire himself out. Brains defeated brawn. But the inscription on Milo's Olympic statue read: 'This magnificent statue represents magnificent Milo, who won seven times at Olympia without his knee ever touching the ground.'[7] So perhaps he did win that sixth adult crown – a quite astonishing achievement, to win as an adult at six successive Olympics. Milo also won so many crowns at the other major games that, like Theogenes, he must have spent a good part of his life travelling around from festival to festival. He was a circuit victor five times. He once went into battle against the neighbouring city of Sybaris wearing all his Olympic crowns, and dressed as Heracles with lion skin and club. He was close to heroization at this point, acting as a talisman for his city's success.

A FAMILY AFFAIR

Theogenes was both a boxer and pankratiast (a combination that became impossible at Olympia after 37 CE, when it was made illegal for one man to enter both contests), Milo a wrestler. We do not know if they inherited their mighty genes or passed them on to their sons, but this was not an uncommon phenomenon in the heavy events. Sons not infrequently followed in their fathers' footsteps. Hipposthenes of Sparta, for instance, was an Olympic wrestling victor six times towards the end of the seventh century BCE, and at the beginning of the sixth his son Etimocles won the same event five times. In the second century CE, Marcus Aurelius Asclepiades, whose father had won at all four crown games, repeated and surpassed his father's achievements at the pankration. But the most famous family of all was that of Diagoras of Rhodes.

Diagoras – another heavy eventer who was said to be of gigantic size – had achieved successes at all the major and many of the minor games, including winning the boxing at Olympia in 464 and being a circuit victor. His eldest son Damagetus won the pankration at Olympia in 452 and then again in 448 – on the same day that his brother Acusilaus won the boxing. They hoisted their father on to their shoulders and carried him through the crowd, who pelted him with flowers and congratulated him on his sons. One spectator even called out that today would be a good day for him to die.[8]

But there were many more good days to come for Diagoras; his family went on to increase their haul of Olympic crowns to nine. His youngest son Dorieus won the pankration at three successive Olympics between 432 and 424. A grandson later won the boxing, while another won the boys' boxing. This latter grandson was Peisirhodus, whom we have already met: it was his mother, one of Diagoras' daughters, who became the only woman other than the priestess of Demeter ever to have been a spectator at the games (see p. 24).

Dorieus, however, should be remembered not just as his father's son. He far surpassed the achievements of his father and brothers. He was an Olympic pankration victor three times, a Pythian victor four times, a Panathenaic victor four times, a Nemean victor seven times, and an Isthmian victor eight times. And this is not to mention all the lesser games where we know he was successful at the toughest of the Greek athletic disciplines. Dorieus was one of the greatest Greek athletes of all time, a household name all over the Greek world.

It seems to have been easier to achieve remarkable feats across the generations in the heavy events than the light ones, perhaps because of the genetic factor I have mentioned and the fact that, over the course of a tiring bout, a heavier contestant had the advantage. Few of these amazing stories feature runners. Still, despite the fact that the Greeks certainly admired the skilful use of brawn that they recognized in athletes such as Theogenes and Milo, they also appreciated those who won by skill alone.

Diodorus of Sicily, writing in the first century BCE, has a telling story about the Athenian Dioxippus, the champion pankratiast at the 336 Olympics. Dioxippus became attached to the court of Alexander the Great and accompanied him on his world-changing campaign of conquest in the east. Many other athletes, and musicians too, accompanied Alexander, so that he could entertain his troops with competitions from time to time; over the course of the eleven-year expedition, he held fourteen such competitions. The following incident took place in what today would be Pakistan, though it was part of 'India' to the Greeks.

> When Alexander had recovered from his wound, he sacrificed to the gods to thank them for saving his life and arranged great banquets for his friends... Among the invited guests was a Macedonian called Coragus, an exceptionally strong man who had often distinguished himself in battle, and, under the influence of alcohol, he challenged Dioxippus to single combat – Dioxippus being an Athenian athlete who had won crowns in the most notable games. Naturally, the guests at the symposium stoked their rivalry, and Dioxippus accepted the challenge. Alexander named a day for the contest, and when the time came for the duel to take place, tens of thousands of men gathered to watch it. The Macedonians and Alexander backed Coragus because he was one of them, while the Greeks were on Dioxippus' side.

Ancient wrestlers had a wide range of techniques. Here, the top wrestler is using a leg hook to pull his opponent over on to his back for a fall.

The Macedonian stepped up for the competition fully armed and arrayed in expensive armour, but the Athenian was naked, with an oiled body, and carried only a moderately sized club. Both men were remarkably well-built and exceptionally strong, so what was about to take place was expected to be little short of a battle between gods. Since the Macedonian's physique and gleaming armour inspired terror, he was taken to be the image of Ares, while Dioxippus, with his exceptional strength, his athletic training and his choice of a club as his weapon, resembled Heracles.

As they closed in on each other, the Macedonian hurled his javelin, but there was still quite a gap between them, and the Greek merely leant aside a little to let it fly harmlessly past. Then the Macedonian couched his pike and advanced, but as soon as he was close the Greek struck the pike with his club and broke it. After these two failures, the Macedonian resorted to his sword, and he was just drawing it when the Greek pounced. With his left hand he seized the Macedonian's right hand, which was drawing the sword, and at the same time he used his other hand to force his opponent off balance and knock him off his feet. Once he was down on the ground, the Greek stood over him with his foot on his neck, raised his club and looked expectantly at the spectators.[9]

Towards the end of the contest, Dioxippus was employing typical pankratiast moves – tripping his opponent and punishing him when he fell. But the story has a sad aftermath. The Macedonians in Alexander's army so resented this Greek victory that they framed Dioxippus as a thief, and the Athenian committed suicide out of shame. No future lightning strike occurred, to save him from relative obscurity.

previous pages
This athlete, in mid-jump, has yet to release his hand-weights. A judge, with his characteristic staff, is assessing the validity and length of the jump.

In no area of human endeavour do the lives and careers of its star performers provide an accurate reflection of the field as a whole. The Olympic festival was the greatest sporting event in the ancient world not because of a few outstanding athletes such as Theogenes and Milo, but because of the thousands of less talented contestants who gave their all over the centuries for the glory of victory, but whose names are largely lost. What the stars and heroes reveal to us, however, is the enormous fervour that the Olympics and other games aroused in both contestants and fans. Athletes competed with actors and singers in ancient Greece for the popular spotlight, but of these three groups only athletes could become more than human.

The passions that sports arouse in their fans can be a source of great joy, but they can also stimulate dark deeds. In the early sixth century CE, factional rioting associated with chariot racing in Constantinople, capital of the Byzantine empire, led to the deaths of thousands of citizens and the destruction of large parts of the city; in the modern era, rioting between fans of the Honduras and El Salvador football teams in 1969 at a time of heightened political tension led to war between the two countries. In the context of the ancient games, as we shall see in the next chapter, the partisan fervour of individual fans was sometimes mirrored by partisan rivalry between states, which was decidedly more dangerous. Politics not infrequently intruded into the games.

Olympic
politics

Olympia was supposed to be neutral ground where members of the Greek elite could meet as equals. This was the Olympic tradition, established early in the history of the festival, but it was not long before it was compromised, becoming more of an ideal than a reality. As long as the focus of the Olympics was chiefly on individuals, the ideal remained attainable, but once states began to see the festival as a site of national rivalry, they inevitably brought their friendships and enmities with them. Moreover, the fact that one state – usually Elis – had control of the site often caused politics to rumble beneath the surface of the festival. The Eleans made sure that their people were scrupulously impartial when it came to judging the competitions (see p. 94), but they could not ignore the fact that their state was also a member of a number of commercial and political networks that encompassed or excluded other Greek states. In this way, the hierarchical pecking order that was recognized by all Greek states and maintained in a number of ways, including warfare and Olympic victory, formed an undercurrent of the festival. The Greeks at Olympia recognized their kinship, but were also not blind to inequalities. The same rivalrous atmosphere permeated the other major athletic festivals as well.

CONCORD, THE OLYMPIC IDEAL

Some intellectuals used Olympia as a platform to call for a greater degree of unity and concord. The certainty of the presence there of a large audience of Greeks made Olympia a perfect location for important political statements. In 324 BCE, for instance, when Alexander the Great wanted to promulgate his notorious Exiles Decree, in which he ordered the Greek states to take back all of their citizens who had been banished for political or other

A typical inscription commemorating the achievements of an athlete, whose statue would have stood on the pedestal. Hundreds of these commemorative statues graced Olympia.

reasons, he had his representative make the announcement at Olympia. Twenty thousand exiles swelled the usual crowd to hear their fate, rejoicing over their imminent return, but knowing that it would cause their states terrible economic and political problems.

Lysias was one of the most talented and famous orators and speech writers of his day. Little remains of the speech that he delivered at Olympia in 388, but the gist of it was that the Greeks should make peace with one another and overthrow Dionysius I, the tyrant of Syracuse, who was aggressively expanding his empire at the time – and who was himself present at the Olympic festival. Lysias, a Syracusan by birth, saw Greek unity not as an end in itself, but as a means to attack a common enemy. The speech was clearly highly inflammatory, and under its influence some of his audience made their way to Dionysius' pavilion and looted it. This was plainly not a call for Greek unity as we would understand it, since Dionysius was as Greek as Lysias.

Two other celebrated orators made Olympic speeches that could also hardly be described as disinterested calls for unity. Both Gorgias of Leontini (in Sicily) in 408, and Isocrates of Athens in 380 (in a pamphlet written as if it were a speech delivered at Olympia, the so-called *Festival Speech*) called on the Greeks to stop fighting one another and unite against the Persians. They were probably envisaging the kind of military alliance that had been formed in 480 to combat the Persian invasion led by Xerxes, nothing more permanent or stable than that. Only a few words survive of Gorgias' speech, but it must have made an impression, because, later, his great-nephew was allowed to erect a statue of the orator at Olympia, the inscribed base of which has survived. Or maybe permission was granted just because Gorgias had become the most famous orator in the Greek world, and therefore a symbol of the kind of success that was celebrated at Olympia.

When we unpack these appeals for unity, they seem pragmatic

rather than idealistic. But at least they were steps in the right direction, and Olympia was a highly appropriate location for such pronouncements, because it was here that, in an earlier period, the notion that there were values that all Greeks shared, wherever they lived, had been given practical form. The Persian invasion of 480 united the Greeks as never before – not numerically, because only thirty-one states resisted the invaders, but in the sense that it increased their awareness that they were all Greeks together. Olympia, being the main place where the Greeks met and mingled, was naturally where this awareness found expression.

It seems that in 476 an international panel was established at Olympia comprising distinguished men from a number of cities – enough that the delegates could be thought to represent 'the Greeks' whose job was to arbitrate disputes and reconcile states before they had recourse to warfare. Archaeologists have unearthed inscriptions that record the decisions reached by this panel in two cases. But only in two cases, making it seem that the experiment was short-lived, and that before long warring Greek states refused to recognize the authority of the panel and stopped submitting their disputes to it.

Despite the failure of this panel, the same spirit of reconciliation is evident in the form of an engraved bronze tablet that was set up in the Altis to mark the thirty-year peace entered into in 445 by the old enemies Athens and Sparta. The treaty was intended to guarantee that a cold war between these two states did not heat up and drag the rest of the Greek world into armed conflict. It failed, and the Peloponnesian War that began in 431 was a result of that failure, but at least the spirit of concord was still being acknowledged at Olympia as an ideal, and preserved as a possibility for future generations.

THE FRINGE FESTIVAL

As well as being a platform for statements of noble political aspirations, Olympia was a place where teachers and intellectuals disseminated their ideas and tried to attract students. The most familiar such figure at the end of the fifth century was Hippias himself, the author of *Olympic Victors*. Since he lived in nearby Elis, it was easy for him to attend every festival, and he used to lecture there on a wide variety of topics and answer questions from his audiences. In his dialogue named after Hippias, Plato has Socrates gently tease the sophist for the way in which he advertised his versatility and polymathy:

> [Socrates talking to Hippias] You said that once you went to Olympia with nothing on your person that you hadn't made yourself. You started with the ring you were wearing, claiming to know how to engrave rings; not only it, but the rest of your jewellery too, and your strigil-and-flask set – all your own work, you said. Then you went on to the shoes you were wearing – cobbled by yourself, you claimed, and your cloak and tunic, woven by yourself. Then you said that although your tunic belt was in the expensive Persian style, you had braided it yourself. But that wasn't all. You had brought epic, tragic and dithyrambic poetry, you said, and many prose speeches in a variety of styles. And you had come equipped not only with exceptional expertise in the areas I have just mentioned, but also in matters of rhythm, intonation, orthography and very many other things besides.[1]

Our picture of the Olympic festival would be incomplete if it did not include the presence of speechifying intellectuals. There was always some form of entertainment going on there – recitals of Homer, public pronouncements by cities wanting to advertise some recent achievement, philosophers and even scientists touting new ideas, artists in various media displaying their

Hera, the divine wife of Zeus, was the patron goddess of the Heraea, the games for girls at Olympia.

wares in the hope of finding patrons. It is possible that in the 420s Herodotus of Halicarnassus read out extracts of the history he was writing of the Persian Wars. Dionysius I, the tyrant of Syracuse, had some of his poetry declaimed at the 388 Olympics. It was mocked and booed by the audience – and this was the same Olympics at which Lysias incited the crowd to raid Dionysius' pavilion (see p. 158). Dionysius was the most powerful man in Europe at the time, but he was not having a good Olympics. This was, if you like, the fringe festival.

GREEKNESS REVISITED

The Olympics fostered a common sense of Greekness, because only certified Greeks were allowed to take part. In fact, this 'certification' (it is not clear what form it took) only began some time in the fifth century. There were two responsible factors. First, by then, Olympia was attracting contestants from much further afield than just the Greek mainland and Magna Graecia, and some of them must have needed vetting. Second, Greek success in the Persian Wars had helped to forge in their minds a supremacist distinction between themselves and inferior 'barbarians',* and it became a matter of pride to affirm one's Greekness in contexts such as the Olympic games.

Having said that, we do not know of any cases where athletes were excluded on the grounds that they were not truly Greek. Although the story that Alexander I of Macedon persuaded the Olympic authorities early in the fifth century that he was Greek is almost certainly false,[2] a later Macedonian king, Philip II, was allowed to take part in the mid-fourth century (he won

---

* Those who did not speak Greek, whose languages sounded to Greek ears like *bar-bar-bar*.

the horse race in 356), and so, not many years later, were other Macedonian noblemen. Macedonians were certainly not fully Greek: they spoke an obscure Greek dialect which was virtually incomprehensible to other Greeks, and retained their own traditions beneath a layer of adopted Greek culture. And then, from the second century BCE, Romans began to be allowed to compete in the games.

So it is not clear quite how seriously the Greeks took the exclusion of 'barbarians'. Nevertheless, they were relatively unified in this respect; even if the distinction between themselves and barbarians was not always clear cut, Greekness lay at the heart of the games and was reaffirmed every time by the requirement, at any rate in the years before the Romans came, that the judges check the ethnicity of contestants. A greater threat to Greek unity and concord at Olympia came from elsewhere.

The fact was that Olympia was invariably under the control of some state or another. As we have seen, it was usually Elis, but others also had their briefer turns. In its earliest days, the festival at Olympia probably needed little organization, but what there was seems to have been in Elean hands. Around 650, however, with the help of the king of Argos, the people of nearby Pisa took over; they burnt down buildings, destroyed and buried old dedications, and effectively recreated the site afresh. Early in the sixth century, it was the Eleans' turn again, and they too made a clean sweep of the site. The temple of Hera, for instance, was taken back to its foundations and rebuilt (with the very size of the new temple advertising Elean control of Olympia); the stadium was given embankments for spectators; the shrine of Pelops was refurbished; the southern area of the Altis was developed for the first time; new administrative buildings were built.

After that, Elean control was secure for a while, and it was under their guidance that the festival prospered and became central to Greek culture. Even when the Spartans inflicted a

overleaf
A late-sixth-century depiction of wrestlers, and one of
the last pictures of athletes wearing loincloths, whereas
at Olympia by that time athletes competed naked.

heavy defeat on them in a war in the last years of the fifth century and removed much of their dependent territory, they were allowed to retain the sanctuary. The Spartans had wanted to take it out of their control and give it to another local state, but in the end they realized that there was no other nearby state, not even Pisa, that could run the festival properly. Spartan influence remained strong, but when the Spartans were critically weakened by warfare in 371,* the Arcadians stepped in and seized the sanctuary. By the late 360s, however, it was back in Elean hands, and again they marked the renewal of their control by significant building and rebuilding work. Thereafter, Elis remained in charge of the sanctuary, although after the conquest of Greece in 338 Macedonian kings could impose their will if they chose. Later, Roman potentates could do the same.

Despite being a festival for all Greeks, Olympia was never under the control of a committee with members drawn from a plurality of Greek states. There was no equivalent of today's International Olympic Committee, and so the festival was bound to be to a certain extent subject to the controlling state's political positions. Many Greek cities had extra-urban sanctuaries, located some way from the city, but within territory they considered theirs. Olympia was in effect an extra-urban sanctuary of Elis. The Eleans provided all the Olympic officials; they established their own administrative buildings on the site; they proclaimed the sacred truce; they were responsible for building the most prominent athletic structures and religious edifices, not least the temple of Zeus itself; they financed the festival and either took the profits or absorbed the losses; they minted Elean coins at Olympia; they displayed copies of Elean treaties and laws in the Altis, often in their own dialect; they had the right to reorganize

---

* In this year Sparta sustained a heavy defeat at Leuctra at the hands of the Thebans, who then strengthened the power of the Arcadians as a counterweight to their Spartan neighbours in the Peloponnese.

dedications, bury redundant ones and refuse offerings. All this proclaimed Elean possession of the sanctuary.

Olympia was thus simultaneously a meeting place for all Greeks and a place where one particular Greek state – with its own interests, alliances and political priorities – presented itself to the world. This dual nature was bound to create tensions. We have already seen that the impartiality of Elean judges could be called into question, but there were more serious consequences – namely the occasional exclusion of Elis's political enemies from the games.

In modern times, such exclusions are familiar, from (to mention only the most famous cases) the ban on Germany after the First and Second World Wars, to the ban on South Africa from 1964 to 1992 because of its apartheid regime. In 420 BCE the Eleans imposed a fine on the Spartans for having infringed the sacred truce and the Spartans refused to pay up. The Eleans rejected the Spartans' appeal, banned them from the games, and even posted armed guards in the Altis to prevent them from sacrificing there. In truth, the issue here was not the alleged non-payment of a fine, but the fact that Elis had just entered into an alliance with Athens, Sparta's mortal enemy at the time.[3]

Undaunted, an elderly and distinguished Spartan called Lichas, who knew that he had a winning team for the four-horse chariot race and was determined to enter it, found a way around the ban by entering it under the name of a citizen of Thebes. When his team won, however, he stepped forward and acknowledged that he, a citizen of Sparta, was the owner. The Eleans had Lichas flogged and driven out of Olympia, and they recorded the victory as Theban, not Spartan.

The ripples continued to spread. A few years later, the Spartan king Agis II was not allowed to perform a sacrifice to Zeus because he wanted to accompany it with a prayer for victory in the ongoing war against Athens. The Elean officials interrupted him, claiming, speciously and provocatively, that by Olympic tradition no Greek should pray for victory over other Greeks. When Sparta attacked Elis at the end of the fifth century, in the savage little war to which I referred above, this was a direct and explicit response to their exclusion from the 420 Olympics, the humiliation of Lichas and the debarment of Agis. And when the Spartans defeated the Eleans in this war, Lichas had a statue erected commemorating his win in 420, despite the Eleans' continuing refusal to acknowledge it.[4]

The 420 Olympics were not the only games to be badly affected as a result of inter-Greek hostilities. When the Arcadians seized Olympia, they entrusted the management of the games of 364 to the Pisatans (who were by now claiming to be the original administrators of the festival), while they provided an armed guard for the Altis. On the second day of the festival – 'they had already held the horse race and the first four events of the pentathlon' – the Eleans and their allies attacked.[5] We can only imagine the panic among the spectators. The site had never been fortified, because the Eleans believed themselves to be inviolable. The battle was indecisive, however, and the Arcadians spent the night reinforcing the Altis strongly enough to deter a second attack by the Eleans on the following day. Before many months had passed, however, the Arcadians were compelled by international diplomatic pressure to give up and the Eleans regained control of Olympia. But since they had not been the managers of the 364 games, they declared them a non-event, not a true Olympics, and deleted them from the official record.

This was perhaps the ugliest occasion when politics marred the festival, but the 175th Olympics in 80 BCE were actually cancelled, probably a unique event in ancient Olympic history. A few years earlier, the Roman general Lucius Cornelius Sulla had so thoroughly plundered the site to pay for his warfare (including a sack of Athens), that it was impossible for the games to be held, except for the boys' stade race. The chronicler Eusebius of Caesarea mournfully records that 'the men did not compete, since Sulla had taken everything to Rome'.[6] The following two festivals were held at Olympia, in a subdued fashion, but things gradually improved and the Olympics revived, not least because Sulla repented and arranged for Olympia to receive the income from a large tract of public farmland.

If we had better evidence, we would surely know of more occasions when lesser political ripples disturbed the surface. In 332, for instance, an Athenian pentathlete called Callippus was fined for attempting to bribe his opponents. The Athenians were convinced that their man was the victim of intrigue and they sent their most distinguished orator, Hyperides, to the Olympic committee to try to persuade it to drop the charge. The Eleans refused, and the Athenians boycotted the games. It is not clear how long this boycott went on – it might even have been over before the games of 328 – but it shows that the threat or practice of boycotting the games is not only a modern phenomenon.

INANIMATE OBJECTS SPEAK

Thanks to Pausanias and archaeology, we have a pretty good idea of the layout of the Altis – the locations of the buildings and other structures, and the statues and larger dedications. It is clear that, in terms of both the positioning of dedications and who was allowed to make them, the Eleans tended to favour their allies over their enemies; it is also clear, however, that they had to respond favourably to a request from one of the great states, even if it was an enemy of theirs. Not infrequently, these inanimate objects communicated a subtle or not-so-subtle political message to viewers.

Olympia was a place where victory was celebrated – military as well as athletic victory. Victories of Greeks over barbarians were commemorated, but so were victories of Greeks over Greeks. Spoils of war were dedicated there or a statue was erected to commemorate a military victory. These dedications were accompanied by inscriptions which gave details of the winners and losers. The inscriptions might be purposely designed to humiliate the losers. In 456, for instance, the Spartans hung a golden shield on the east pediment of the temple of Zeus to commemorate a victory over the Athenians and their allies, and the accompanying inscription sarcastically described the shield as a 'gift' from those they defeated. The message there was obvious, and by donating a golden shield rather than a real one taken from their enemies (which was normal practice), the Spartans cleverly got around the Elean habit of periodically clearing the site of smaller, less valuable dedications to make room for further batches.

So the shield and its inscription remained in place for many years – a fact of which the Messenians, enemies of Sparta, took advantage a few decades later. Paeonius of Mende's Victory, commissioned by the Messenians for their defeat of the Spartans in the 420s (see p. 32) and perched on top of a towering column, was oriented directly to face the Spartans' golden shield. Thus, for as long as the monuments survived, the Messenian Victory would tower over the Spartans' shield, heaping further shame on Sparta for a rare and shocking defeat. No doubt the Eleans were aware of what they were doing when they assigned the Messenians that location for their monument; this was the time when Elean relations with Sparta were fast deteriorating, leading before long to the Spartan exclusion from the 420 Olympics.

Although Olympia was supposed to be a place where Greeks met Greeks as equals, it did not necessarily generate warm feelings of kinship. By means of its statues, it functioned as a place

This statue of the pankratiast Agias of Pharsalus,
victor at Olympia in 484, is typical of the idealized,
non-realistic kind of commemorative statue.

of memory, but the memories were not always happy ones. Local identities were just as likely to be reinforced as any sense of shared Greekness. And there were no monuments to any pan-Greek alliance against a common foe, because that never happened. Even the temple of Zeus, by far the largest structure in the Altis and dedicated to the father of all the Greek gods, commemorated Greek-on-Greek conflict – namely an Elean victory over Pisa. The Eleans also erected an enormous bronze statue of Zeus, 9 metres (30 ft) tall, to mark their victory over the Arcadians in the late 360s. We know of monuments commemorating the victories of Megara over Corinth, Locri over Croton, Methana over Sparta, Sicyon over Athens, Syracuse over Acragas – and many more.

The kinds of tensions between states that these monuments exacerbated were bound to be further increased by local loyalties during the games. It is very likely that visitors from the same state sat or stood together as spectators, and created a lot of noise in favour of their home state and to the detriment of others, while the others were of course doing the same. And announcements by the town crier of the names and state affiliations of competitors and victors would have offered additional opportunities for noisy displays of tribalism.

In the later fifth century, however, as we have seen in the case of Agis II of Sparta, the Eleans seem to have made an effort to put an end to the habit of celebrating inter-Greek wars. Statues commemorating athletic victory took the place of those commemorating military victory. The Greeks still found subtle ways to disrespect their enemies – the Spartans' athletic statues came to be more or less surrounded by Elean ones, for instance – but it became rarer. And by the third century, the Greeks were more politically unified anyway, albeit under Macedonian leadership, so the impulse to disrespect their neighbours died down.

When Philip II of Macedon formed the Greeks into a league in 337 BCE, he arranged for it to meet in rotation at the sites of the four crown games; power no longer lay with the fractious city states of Greece, and international concord could become a genuine goal. Athletics became valued more as entertainment and less as a way to demonstrate political superiority. Much of the earlier history of the Olympics, however, was undoubtedly characterized by belligerent rivalry between states, their supporters and their athletes. The Stoic philosopher Epictetus mentioned noise as one of the many discomforts of Olympia. It is very likely that during the games Olympia resounded with rowdy and partisan cries, and not a few fist fights. State rivalries spilled over into the stadium and the hippodrome.

The decline
and revival of
the Olympics

One of the chief difficulties in trying to gain an overview of any aspect of ancient Greek history is the patchiness of the sources. As far as the Olympics are concerned, our two most important literary sources – Pausanias and Philostratus – were both writing well inside the Roman period, and it is difficult to tell how much of what they say about events or athletic techniques applies to an earlier period, or to what extent they are putting forward idiosyncratic views. Otherwise, references in Greek literature to the Olympics tend to be asides, not the central concern of the author, and badly need supplementing with the evidence of archaeology, inscriptions and vase painting. Moreover, after the Macedonian conquest of the east the attention of historians and writers shifted away from Greek affairs. This process only accelerated after the Roman conquest of Greece, which was complete by 146 BCE. Writers naturally focused on the great affairs of the eastern kings and on Rome, not on the backwater that Greece had become.

The worst consequence of all this for writing a history of the ancient Olympics is that although the games continued for centuries after the Macedonian and then Roman conquests of Greece, and remained popular, we know less and less about them as the decades go by. Our most important resource for these centuries is archaeology. The record shows that Olympia continued to attract the attention of wealthy and powerful benefactors, and that the Eleans continued to have money to spend. New buildings went up and old ones were repaired, though the emphasis was less on religious building (which was arguably already complete) and more on athletic structures and infrastructure. King Herod of Judaea – the infamous Herod of the New Testament – paid for the entire games in 12 BCE. In the second century CE, the wealthy Athenian banker Herodes Atticus ran an aqueduct from a spring 2.5 miles (4 km) distant and provided the Altis for the first time with ample, easily accessible water. Emperor Nero was another benefactor. This is just a small sample of the benefactions Olympia received.

Clearly, in the late republican and early imperial period, Romans and others were concerned to maintain and improve the site and the festival – although the concern of benefactors was also to boost their own prestige by having their names attached to a place as famous as Olympia. The Romans admired Greek culture in almost all its manifestations, and were eager to absorb and support it. But the water is somewhat muddied by the fact that the site seems to have become more liable to flooding, which may indicate a degree of neglect. Moreover, the dedication of statues declined in the last couple of centuries BCE. Does this indicate less interest from contestants, or poverty (the Roman conquest had left Greece very badly off), or just a change of fashion?

Then again, for at least 250 years from the beginning of the first century BCE all the winners of the equestrian events that we know of (though there are very many gaps) came from Elis, apart from the occasional Roman dignitary. The equestrian events may even have been cancelled altogether for several Olympiads in the first centuries CE; at any rate, we hear of very few winners. This could mean that horse owners from elsewhere were too hard up to participate at Olympia – but it might mean that they were simply focusing on other games. Travellers by boat to Olympia from the east coast of mainland Greece had to round Cape Malea, at the southeastern corner of the Peloponnese, which was always a fearsome prospect in ancient times; it was easier to sail to Asia Minor, where there were by now many prestigious and rich games to be entered, and there were major new games on mainland Greece itself as well.

On the whole, there seems no good reason to think that, up until the end of the second century CE, Olympia went into much of a decline. In fact, there was a resurgence of interest in the games in the second century CE. However, it is possible that

overleaf
A few fragmentary stretches remain of the defensive wall erected in the 260s CE, reusing stones from other buildings (see p. 181).

the splendour of the Altis, on which wealthy Romans showered money, had become more of an attraction than the athletics. It is clear, at any rate, that the visitors were still coming. The most dramatic gesture by an intellectual in the history of the entire games came in 165 CE, the 236th Olympics. A Cynic philosopher called Peregrinus, a former Christian, who lived as a beggar and a tramp (as true Cynics were supposed to), had announced at the previous festival his intention to immolate himself on a funeral pyre as a form of protest against the corruption of the world. And so he did. He clearly wanted maximum publicity for the speech he gave, outlining his reasons for suicide – and it was still the Olympics that could gain him the largest ready-made audience, for both his words and his suicide.[1]

The most famous orator of his day, Dio Chrysostom ('the golden-tongued'), considered it worthwhile to give a speech at Olympia towards the end of the first century CE; Emperor Nero had considered it worth buffing his ego there in the 60s. The games were still popular enough for Pausanias, writing in the second century CE, to devote a full 20 per cent of his *Description of Greece* to Olympia, knowing that his readers would appreciate it. It is likely that Olympia in the early imperial period had become a more comfortable place to visit, and that the athletes one saw there were more professional than their predecessors. There was certainly far more prize money available for them at festivals around the world, especially for the heavy events, which were particularly admired by the Romans. The weight of tradition ensured that the games remained substantially the same, though more polished, more hygienic (the Romans were keen on building bath houses), and more leisurely too, since they occupied six rather than five days.

After the end of the second century CE, however, the festival went into decline. Some buildings were allowed to fall into disrepair, statues were removed from the site and visitor numbers declined. Athletes were still proud to take part and to win, but the Olympics no longer enjoyed its former cachet and the site became a little shabby. The pagan gods of Greece were now less attractive to many than Mithras, Isis, or even the new god, Jesus Christ. We cannot even be sure that games were held at every Olympiad. The only major building work was the erection for the first time of fortifications, probably in the 260s, to guard against the possibility of attack from Gothic invaders; the stones and materials for this work were gained by demolishing other structures in the Altis.

By the second half of the fourth century CE, games were closing all over the Mediterranean world, probably because individuals were less interested in financing such projects, and states had too many other demands on their revenues. The games were officially closed by Emperor Theodosius in 393; it may have taken a couple of decades for his edict to take effect, but the Olympic festival was already in a parlous condition. The final blow came with the destruction of the temple of Zeus by earthquakes in the sixth century CE. The fallen columns still make dramatic viewing for visitors to the site, but the failure to rebuild the iconic temple shows that the ancient Olympics had been consigned to history. The site was converted into a Christian village, whose inhabitants availed themselves of what remained of the splendid structures of the past.

THE BARON'S VISION

The revival of the Olympic games at the end of the nineteenth century was due entirely to the vision of one man. Baron Pierre de Coubertin (1863–1937) was a dapper Frenchman with a splendid moustache, and an admirer of the kind of English education he

overleaf
The earthquake-toppled columns of the temple of Zeus
still testify to its size and former magnificence.
The standing column is a modern reconstruction.

associated with Thomas Arnold and that we associate with *Tom Brown's Schooldays*, with its combination of sport and intellectual pursuits – a combination which educationalists at the time took to reflect and perpetuate ancient Greek values. Looking back at the ancient Olympics through rose-tinted glasses, they saw the event as fostering the ideal of the gifted amateur, which we have seen to be not strictly true. Their vision – Coubertin's vision – lasted long: professional sportsmen and women, who make money from their skills, were finally allowed to compete in the Olympics only in 1988, and then only at the discretion of the governing bodies of each discipline. Over the following decades, almost all governing bodies have agreed to allow professionals into the Olympics.

The idealistic baron believed that the ancient Greek world had seen a perfect amalgam of mind and muscle, from which all the virtues effortlessly flowed. He was not alone in wanting to see the ancient games revived, but he was the only one who had the determination to see it through. He had several sources of inspiration. The German excavations of Olympia from the 1870s had greatly impressed him and first sown the idea. Then there had been games in England, Germany, Greece and elsewhere which called themselves 'Olympic'. Most of them were scarcely more than rural fairs with pretensions, but the Greek ones (held in Athens and sponsored by the millionaire Evangelis Zappas) had, as in ancient times, attracted contestants from Greek communities abroad, as well as on the mainland. In these 'Olympics', however, athletics came second to exhibitions of Greek agricultural produce. But Coubertin wanted to make the Olympics the greatest sporting event in the modern world, as it had been in the ancient world.

So Coubertin set about reviving the games as a kind of modernization of the putative ancient Olympic ideals of unity, equality and concord. Coubertin did not naively believe that

Baron Pierre de Coubertin (1863–1937), the prime mover of the revival of the Olympics in the modern era.

reviving the games would automatically lead to world peace, but he did believe that it would foster respect, as an important first step, and this was the ideal for which he strove all his life and on which he exhausted his family fortune. After his death, his body was buried in Lausanne, but his heart was cut out and taken to Olympia, where it is buried under a monument in the grounds of the local Olympic headquarters.

By the early 1890s, Coubertin had become an influential member of French sporting and educational circles, and had travelled widely to witness at first hand the state and status of sports in other countries. America opened his eyes to the immense popularity of sporting events, and the 1889 Universal Exhibition in Paris showed him how attractive and emotionally powerful international public spectacles could be. In 1894 he hijacked the meeting of the main French umbrella organization for sports, and invited sportsmen and educationalists from seventy-nine countries around the world to a Congress of Amateurs to discuss the establishment of international Olympic festivals for amateur sportsmen (not yet women).

All of Coubertin's proposals were passed; the games were to be held at four-yearly intervals and were to continue the spirit of the ancient games rather than being exact imitations (so that athletes would not compete unclothed, for example, and a different set of events would be involved). Dimitrios Vikelas of Athens was appointed the head of the first International Olympic Committee, but after only two years Coubertin himself took over and held the post until his retirement in 1925. Much of the world's press thought the idea a non-starter. Sport was still a very marginal occupation in the late nineteenth century, largely limited to Britain, America, and the British overseas colonies, with less penetration into Europe.

The appointment of Vikelas was a clever move. Coubertin wanted the first new games, now scheduled for 1896, to be held in

Athens, for sound symbolic reasons, but he knew that Greece was a poor country – it had declared bankruptcy only a few years previously – and expected official opposition. He needed a local ally, and Vikelas had the stature to help. King George I of Greece gave his blessing, but the government was another matter. Prime Minister Harilaos Trikoupis had entered upon his third term of office with promises of fiscal conservatism and continued to argue that his country could not afford to host the games. Coubertin went to Athens. He cunningly won over the press and more members of the royal family to his side, and then, pointing to existing sporting facilities in Athens, he concocted a ludicrously low budget for the whole event. He was not above being somewhat economical with the truth.

Trikoupis bowed to popular pressure; holding the games would, after all, be a good way for Greece to show its ongoing willingness to Europeanize. He soon retired to France (and he was to die, by coincidence, just a few days before the festival), but the Greeks were now committed to the project. It became clear, however, that it would cost far more than Coubertin had said. Gifts of money poured in from wealthy Greek expatriates. One particularly well-off Alexandrian Greek, Giorgios Averoff, personally guaranteed all the money needed to refurbish the ancient Panathenaic stadium with marble and wooden seating. Special postage stamps were issued to raise further funds.

Coubertin was hugely energetic. He drew up the invitation list of individuals and athletic clubs, tried to patch up hostilities between countries, and worked out the programme of the festival. Once everything was in place, he made a long-delayed pilgrimage to Olympia. He later said: 'I became aware in this sacred place of the enormity of the task I had undertaken in proclaiming five months earlier the restoration of the Olympic games after a gap of 1,500 years, and I glimpsed all the hazards which would dog me on the way.' But none of

the hazards proved insurmountable, and the games went ahead as planned.

THE 1896 OLYMPICS

The games opened on 6 April. Banners in the streets of Athens proclaimed: 'The Olympic Games, 776 BC–1896 AD'. Music filled the air. There were an estimated 100,000 spectators – one of the largest gatherings of people for peaceful purposes the world at the time had ever seen. An American visitor, Burton Holmes, wrote: 'The sight is one which thrills us, one the like of which has never before been witnessed in our modern age. The first glimpse of the crowded Stadium is to be numbered among the great sensations of a lifetime.'[2]

Flags and statues adorned the stadium. The entry of the Greek royal family was greeted by a tumultuous ovation. There was no initial procession of the athletes, as nowadays, and no Olympic flame (which was introduced for the 1936 Olympics), but hundreds of Athenian schoolboys put on a gymnastic display. The famous five-ring symbol was also nowhere to be seen; it was invented in 1913 by Coubertin to represent the five main regions of the world. The king declared the games open, and then the Olympic hymn, written by Kostis Palamas and set to music by Spyros Samaras, was sung. It was repeated at the end of the games, as well – and finally became the official Olympic anthem in 1956, at the Melbourne Olympics.

The 1896 Olympics were an all-male affair, like their ancient counterpart; the first women's events were introduced in 1900 (golf and lawn tennis), and it is only gradually, over many Olympiads, that women's sports have become fully represented. After all, on the ancient Greek model competitiveness was a male prerogative. The music and spectacles, although only a pale reflection of the razzamatazz that attends the games nowadays, were more impressive than any of the events, since only the Americans and some of the English believed in pre-contest training; moreover, the cinder track was too soft, and the ancient stadium too tight at the turns, to encourage fast times. Only nine events were represented: track and field, cycling, fencing, gymnastics, shooting, swimming, weightlifting and wrestling. Rowing and sailing were cancelled due to the bad weather that plagued the whole games; the equestrian events had been dropped at the preparatory stage as being too expensive. There were 311 participants, 230 of whom were Greek. Although the Americans were not the largest foreign team (they were outnumbered by both the French and the Germans), they were the only ones to field a reasonable number of men who were both well equipped and well trained, and so they won a disproportionate number of the events. Winners were awarded silver medals.

The climax came on the fifth day with the marathon race, run over a roughly 25-mile (40 km) course from the village of Marathon, northeast of Athens, to the stadium in the city, and heralded as the first-ever revival of an ancient run (see Appendix, pp. 198–201). No one quite knew what to expect. Would athletes even be capable of completing the course? There were seventeen starters. A little tampering with the rules had allowed a Greek farmer called Spyros Louis to enter, even though, since he was not a gentleman, he was not a member of an athletic club. Fifty thousand people packed the stadium and thousands more lined the route. The largely Greek audience had politely clapped and cheered the string of American victories over the course of the previous days, but they longed for a Greek victor in this event above all.

The marathon started at 2 p.m. A German cyclist brought news to the stadium that Edwin Flack, an Australian competing

overleaf
Three men (identities unknown) compete in the 1896 marathon, which was the first time people had raced over such a distance.

for imperial Britain, was well in front. But then definite news arrived that a Greek was in the lead. Shortly afterwards, sunburnt and covered in dust, Louis entered the stadium, showing hardly any signs of tiredness. He had run an intelligent race, keeping well back, and apparently even stopping for a glass of wine at one point. The athletes who went out hard in the afternoon sun (almost the only sun these games saw) dropped like flies on the uphill sections. Louis came in seven minutes ahead of the second runner, who was in turn half a minute ahead of the next. All three were Greeks. The third-placed runner, however, was later disqualified: he had accepted a lift on a cart for some of the course. The winning time – and a world record, of course, since this was the first marathon race – was two hours, fifty-eight and a half minutes.

The crowd erupted in a frenzy of flag- and hat-waving, shouting and shedding tears of joy. The band was forced to play the Greek national anthem over and over again. Prince Constantine and his younger brother George flanked Louis as he ran the last 200 metres in the stadium, with bouquets of flowers raining down on him. Even the king was on his feet and waving his hat in the air. Then the princes raised the victor on to their shoulders. Coubertin always remembered the scene as one of the most extraordinary spectacles he had ever seen.

Only one Greek paper, a few days later, complained about the bending of the rules that had allowed a farmer to compete, rather than only the social equals of the representatives of other countries. In ancient times, as we have seen, an Olympic victor would be heaped with honours and privileges on his return home. Pretty much the same happened to Louis. In an ecstasy of patriotism, women tried to press gold chains and watches on him, and men substantial amounts of cash; others offered free meals for a year, coffee twice a day for life, whatever he wanted. One woman (or so we hear) had even offered to marry the marathon winner, if he was a Greek – but the offer was withdrawn when she found that it was a farmer who had won. Louis refused almost all these gifts. He was a self-effacing young man, and he never traded on his great fame. Forty years later, however, he agreed to lead the Greek team in the opening procession of the Berlin Olympics. In the meantime, his name had become proverbial: 'to do a Louis' means in modern Greek to make a special effort. And when the Olympics returned to Athens in 2004, the main stadium was named after him.

The snobbery and elitism that were part of the 1896 games were inevitable – and a true reflection of the ancient games. Coubertin's conception of the games was that they should be strictly for amateurs, but that restricted them, in effect, to the moneyed elite who were members of athletic clubs around the world and who had spare time to train. This was the era of the 'gentleman amateur'. One is reminded of the iconic scene from the 1981 film *Chariots of Fire*, about the 1924 Olympics, in which Lord Andrew Lindsay, played by Nigel Havers, practises the high hurdles on his estate with glasses of champagne balanced on the hurdles against any contact. This is hardly an exaggeration of the reality.

Coubertin felt that the Athenian Olympics had proved his thesis that the games could foster fellowship and ultimately peace between nations. He had seen displays of patriotism without nationalism, of honest rivalry and mutual respect, and of shared enthusiasm for physical prowess. Since he projected all these values back on to the ancient Olympics, he felt that he had done what he set out to do: he had revived the ancient games. He had given modern athletes a platform on which to display excellence, just as the ancient Olympics had done.

The 1896 games were declared a great success, and the Greek royal family wanted them to have a permanent home in Athens. The king described Greece as 'the mother and nurse of athletic

games in antiquity'. The attempt to retain the games in Athens was supported even by the entire American team. But Coubertin's vision was of a truly global event, circulating among major cities of the world; that was his updating of the internationalism of the ancient games. He replaced Vikelas at the head of the International Olympic Committee, and from this position of authority he overrode the objections and ensured that the 1900 games were scheduled for Paris.

As a compromise, Coubertin suggested that Athens might host all-Greek games at four-yearly intervals between the international Olympics. In the event, these intercalary games took place only once, in 1906, and it was just as well they did, because the 1900 and 1904 Olympics, respectively in Paris and St Louis, were not at all successful. Steam was beginning to run out of the Olympic movement – but the 1906 event was a great success, the 1908 Olympics in London were good enough to keep the public's interest alive, and then thanks to the brilliant 1912 Stockholm Olympics the Olympic movement built up enough impetus to see it through the First World War – and on into the future.

Spyros Louis, on the right, wearing a fustanella, stands with other Greek medallists at the conclusion of the 1896 games.

Appendix

THE LEGEND OF THE MARATHON RUN

It is commonly believed that the marathon run was invented in commemoration of the feat of an ancient runner. Unfortunately, this is doubly wrong: there was no such ancient run, and the marathon distance (26.2 miles / 42.2 km) is only a little over 100 years old. It is true, of course, that there was a famous battle on the Marathon Plain, not far northeast of Athens. In 490 BCE the Persians invaded Greece to punish the Athenians for having supported rebels from the vast Persian empire; to everyone's surprise, the outnumbered Athenian troops defeated the Persians at the Battle of Marathon.

The climax of the revived Olympic games in Athens in 1896 was the marathon race, run on the fifth day of the games, over a roughly 25-mile (40 km) course from the village of Marathon to the stadium in the city (which was the ancient Panathenaic stadium, newly refurbished by a wealthy expatriate Greek). The popular press heralded the event as the first 'revival' of the run of the ancient messenger who carried the news of the Greek victory from the Battle of Marathon to Athens in 490 BCE.

But in fact there is no good evidence for this ancient run. Herodotus of Halicarnassus, the historian of the Persian Wars, tells a story about a runner called Philippides or Pheidippides who was sent from Athens to Sparta (about 140 miles or 225 km) to ask the Spartans for help against the imminent Persian landing at Marathon. In other words, Herodotus, our closest source (writing about sixty years after the battle), does not mention anyone running a distance of 25 miles or so, let alone a run to or from the village or battle of Marathon.*

---

*   Pheidippides' run is still remembered in the annual running of the Spartathlon, every year since 1984.

The fake marathon story only surfaces, as far as our evidence goes, 600 years after the battle in an essay by Plutarch of Chaeronea. He says that an Athenian soldier called Eucles ran in armour from the battlefield to Athens, 'burst through the doors of the leaders' meeting-room, and had time only to say, "Greetings! Victory is ours!", before expiring'. Then a somewhat later writer, the witty belle-lettrist Lucian of Samosata, tells the same story as Plutarch, but with the name taken from Herodotus.[1] This amalgamated version, perpetuated by, for instance, Robert Browning in his 1879 poem 'Pheidippides', is the one which has become familiar to us.

So there was no ancient marathon run, and the first modern marathons that were run covered about 25 miles (40 km). This was the case not just at the 1896 Athens Olympics, but also at the 1900 and 1904 Olympics (and at the 1906 intercalary Olympics). Even the Boston Marathon, which started as an annual event in 1897, was run at first over this distance. Twenty-five miles is a nice, round figure, but the current distance of 26 miles and 385 yards is an anomaly; it does not make a round number in kilometres either. How, then, did it come about?

In 1908 London was chosen (at the last minute, following the withdrawal of Rome) as the host of the Olympics. The stadium where many of the events were held, and where the marathon was to finish, was in Shepherd's Bush, a district of west London. It was decided to begin the marathon out to the west of London, and King Edward VII and the royal family put pressure on the organizers to start it at Windsor, so that they could get a good view from their castle. The organizers were only too happy to comply with His Majesty's request. There was only one snag: starting the race at the foot of Windsor Castle would lengthen it by a little over a mile... and that is how the distance became 26.2 miles. Shortly after the games, the international sporting community accepted this as the official distance.

Timeline

BCE

*c.*1400
First human occupation of future site of Olympia.

776
Traditional date for the first games at Olympia, consisting only of running races.

*c.*750–480
'Archaic' period of Greek history.

708
Combat sports introduced at the Olympic games.

680
Equestrian events introduced at the Olympic games.

676
Pisa gains control of Olympia.

c 650
Nudity becomes the norm for athletes at the Olympic games.

632
Boys' events introduced at the Olympic games.

*c.*590
Elis regains control of Olympia.

586
Overhaul of Pythia festival of Delphi to bring it in line with the Olympics.

580
Isthmian games established near Corinth.

573
Nemean games established; festival circuit of 'crown' games complete.

566
Upgrading of Panathenaea festival of Athens to international status.

*c.*550
Heraea festival reorganized at Olympia and includes races for unmarried girls.

*c.*520
Milo of Croton active.

518–*c.*440
Life of Pindar of Boeotia, praise-poet.

490
Battle of Marathon

480–479
Persian invasion of Greece.

479–323
'Classical' period of Greek history.

476
Establishment of short-lived international board at Olympia to arbitrate interstate relations.

c.460
Construction of the temple of Zeus at Olympia.

c.450
Theogenes of Thasos active.

c.435
Pheidias of Athens designs statue of Zeus at Olympia.

431–404
Peloponnesian War between Athens and Sparta.

420
Spartans excluded from the Olympics for political reasons.

408
Gorgias of Leontini addresses the Olympic audience.

c.410
Hippias of Elis active.

402–400
Spartan war against Elis.

396
First female victor at Olympics (Cynisca of Sparta).

392
Number of Olympic judges (*Hellanodikai*) raised to ten.

388
Lysias of Syracuse/Athens addresses the Olympic audience.

380
Isocrates of Athens addresses the Olympic audience.

364
Violence erupts in the sacred precinct of Olympia; Elis regains control of Olympia from a brief Pisatan ascendancy.

356
Philip of Macedon allowed to take part in the Olympics.

c.330
New (third) stadium built.

323
Death of Alexander the Great.

323–30
'Hellenistic' period of Greek history.

146 BCE–1453 CE
Roman imperial period of Greek history.

80
Olympic games cancelled; only one boys' race run at Olympia itself.

27
The Roman emperor Augustus adds the Actia to the circuit of crown games.

12
King Herod of Judaea funds the games.

CE

67
The Roman emperor Nero hijacks the games.

c.160–170
Pausanias travelling and compiling his *Description of Greece*.

165
The philosopher Peregrinus' Olympic suicide.

c.170–c.245
Life of Philostratus, author of *On Athletic Exercise*.

393
The Roman emperor Theodosius the Great orders the closure of all non-Christian sites and festivals.

1766
Rediscovery of site of Olympia by Richard Chandler.

1821–32
Greek War of Independence against Ottoman empire.

1829
Temple of Zeus uncovered by French expedition.

1859
The first of four 'Olympic festivals' put on in Athens and funded by Evangelis Zappas, featuring agricultural innovations more than sport.

1860–4
William Penny Brookes runs the Shropshire Olympian Games.

1863–1937
Life of Baron Pierre de Coubertin.

1866
William Penny Brookes's National Olympian Association puts on games in London.

1875–81
First series of annual digs at Olympia by German Archaeological Institute.

1894
Foundation of International Olympic Committee by Coubertin.

1896
First modern Olympics held in Athens.

1988
Olympics opened up to professional sportsmen and sportswomen.

Notes

PROLOGUE

1 Pindar, *Pythian Odes*, 8.86–7.

2 'The Sporting Spirit', *Tribune* (London), December 1945; available at www.orwell. ru/library/articles/spirit/english/e_ spirit.

3 Tyrtaeus, fragment 12 West; Euripides, fragment 282 Nauck, from the lost *Autolycus*, part of a longer paragraph criticizing athletics.

1 SACRED OLYMPIA

1 Pindar's *Pythian Odes* 2 and 3 were also commissioned by Hiero.

2 Aelian, *On the Nature of Animals*, 5.17.

3 *Epigraphes Kato Makedonias* 1.398.

4 Diogenes Laertius, *Lives of Eminent Philosophers*, 1.39.

5 Herodotus, *Histories*, 8.144.

6 Philostratus, *On Athletic Exercise*, 17.

7 Pausanias, *Description of Greece*, 5.11.

8 Homer, *Iliad*, 6.208, 11.783.

9 Athenaeus, *The Learned Banquet*, 1.5e.

10 This particular curse tablet, dating from Roman times, was found not at Olympia, but in the ancient agora of Athens, but there is no reason to think that the practice did not go on at Olympia as well. D. Jordan, 'Fourteen Defixiones from a Well near the Southwest Corner on the Athenian Agora', *Hesperia*, 54 (1985), 205–55.

2 ORIGINS

1 Pausanias, *Description of Greece*, 5.7–8. For alternative dates for the start of the Olympics, see P. Christesen, *Olympic Victor Lists and Ancient Greek History* (Cambridge University Press, 2007), Appendix 14.

2 Pindar, *Olympian Odes*, 10; Aulus Gellius, *Attic Nights*, 1.1.

3 Plutarch, *Moralia*, fragment 7 Sandbach.

4 Pindar, *Olympian Odes*, 1; Pausanias, *Description of Greece*, 5.17.7; Apollodorus, *Epitome*, 2.3–9.

5 Thucydides, *History*, 5.11.1.

6 See the discussion in T. Scanlon, *Eros and Greek Athletics* (Oxford University Press, 2002), chapter 3.

7 See e.g. D. Sansone, *Greek Athletics*

and the Genesis of Sport (University of
California Press, 1988).

8 A. Patay-Horvath, The Origins of the
Olympic Games (Archaeolingua, 2015).

9 Strabo, Geography, 8.3.30.

10 See especially C. Morgan, Athletes and
Oracles: The Transformation of Olympia
and Delphi in the Eighth Century BC
(Cambridge University Press, 1990).

11 Homer, Odyssey, 8.145–64.

12 Plato, Laws, 807c.

13 Aristotle, Rhetoric, 1365a 26–7. Ephesus
inscription: I.Eph. 2005 (see also I.Eph.
1416). Papyrus: Miller, Arete, no. 207.

14 Isocrates, The Team of Horses, 33.

15 Xenophon, Memorabilia, 3.7.1.

---

3   SPORT AND SOCIETY IN
     ANCIENT GREECE

1 Livy, History of Rome, 33.32.2.

2 Herodotus, Histories, 8.26.

3 Xenophanes, fragment 2 Diels/Kranz.

4 Plato, Apology of Socrates, 36d–e. For
Isocrates, see e.g. Letter, 8.5.

5 Herodotus, Histories, 5.71; Thucydides,
History, 1.126.

6 Pindar, Nemean Odes, 5.1–3.

7 Supplementum Epigraphicaum Graecum,
47.1745.

8 I Maccabees 1.14.

9 Pindar, Olympian Odes, 9.94; Dio
Chrysostom, Orations, 28.5.

10 Plato, Charmides, 155c.

11 Theognidea, 1335–6.

12 Plato, Phaedrus, 255c ff.

13 Plato, Symposium, 182a–d. The basic
book on the subject is K. Dover, Greek
Homosexuality (2nd ed., with new
introductions, Bloomsbury, 2016).

14 Pseudo-Xenophon, The Constitution of
the Athenians, 1.13.

15 Aeschines, Against Timarchus, 138;
Plutarch, Solon, 1.

16 Miller, Arete, no. 185.

17 Pindar, Olympian Odes, 8.54–66.

18 Charmis: Sextus Julius Africanus (3rd
century CE), Chronography, under the
year 668. Avoidance of sex: Plato, Laws,
839e–840a. Cleitomachus: Plutarch,
Moralia, 710d (Table Talk); Aelian,
Historical Miscellany, 3.30, On the
Nature of Animals, 6.1.

19 Philostratus, On Athletic Exercise, 20–3.

20 Cross-training by swimming:
Philostratus, On Athletic Exercise, 43.
Galen, On Exercise with a Small Ball, On
the Preservation of Health, 2.9.

21 Epictetus, Discourses, 3.15.2–3.

22 Pausanias, Description of Greece, 1.44.1.
The second version is from Isidore of
Seville, Etymologiae, 18.17.2, written in
the seventh century CE.

23 Aristotle, Politics, 1297a25–31.

4 THE OLYMPIC FESTIVAL

1 Second Hypothesis to Demosthenes, *On the Dishonest Embassy*, 3.

2 Xenophon, *Hellenica*, 4.1.40; Pausanias, *Description of Greece*, 6.2.10–11.

3 Diodorus of Sicily, *Library of History*, 1.95. A similar story in Herodotus, *Histories*, 2.160.

4 Miller, *Arete*, no. 81.

5 Miller, *Arete*, no. 84.

6 This table is based on Pausanias, *Description of Greece*, 5.8.6–5.9.1, who followed Hippias' dating.

7 Timaeus of Tauromenium, fragment 26a Jacoby.

5 THE EVENTS

1 Pausanias, *Description of Greece*, 6.13.9.

2 Xenophon, *Agesilaus*, 9.6.

3 Miller, *Arete*, no. 98b.

4 Sophocles, *Electra*, 696–756.

5 Aristotle, *The Art of Rhetoric*, 1361b7–11.

6 The two athletes are Chionis of Sparta, in the seventh century, as recorded in the second century CE by Zenobius, *Proverbs*, 6.23, and Phayllus of Croton, early in the fifth century, as recorded in an epigram (*Palatine Anthology*, Appendix, 3.297).

7 Pausanias, *Description of Greece*, 8.40.1.

8 Philostratus, *On Athletic Exercise*, 10; Eustathius, 1324.18.

9 Dio Chrysostom, *Orations*, 28–9.

10 *Supplementum Epigraphicum Graecum*, 22.354 (second century CE).

11 Aelian, *Historical Miscellany*, 10.19.

12 Theocritus, *Idylls*, 22.27–134.

13 Pausanias, *Description of Greece*, 6.4.3.

14 Pindar, *Isthmian Odes*, 4.48.

15 Pausanias, *Description of Greece*, 5.21.18; the event took place at the Olympics of 25 CE.

16 Pausanias, *Description of Greece*, 5.12.8.

17 Pausanias, *Description of Greece*, 5.16.

6 HEROES AND VICTORS

1 L. Moretti, *Iscrizione Agonistiche Greche* (Signorelli, 1953), 59.

2 Pausanias, *Description of Greece*, 6.11.

3 Pausanias, *Description of Greece*, 6.6; Strabo, *Geography*, 6.1.5.

4 J. Ebert, *Griechische Epigramme auf Sieger an gymnischen und hippischen Agonen* (Berlin, 1972), no. 37.

5 Pausanias, *Description of Greece*, 6.5.

6 Pausanias, *Description of Greece*, 6.14.5–8; Athenaeus, *The Learned Banquet*, 10.412f.

7 Simonides, *Epigrams*, 25 Page.

8 Pausanias, *Description of Greece*, 6.7.

9 Diodorus of Sicily, *Library of History*, 17.100.

7   OLYMPIC POLITICS

1   Plato, *Hippias Minor*, 368b–d.

2   Herodotus, *Histories*, 5.22.

3   Thucydides, *History*, 5.49–50.

4   Pausanias, *Description of Greece*, 6.2.2–3;
     Xenophon, *Hellenica*, 3.2.22.

5   Xenophon, *Hellenica*, 7.4.28–32.

6   Eusebius, *Chronica*, 462–3 Christesen
     (early fourth century CE).

8   THE DECLINE AND REVIVAL
OF THE OLYMPICS

1   Lucian, *On the Death of Peregrinus*

2   Burton Holmes, *The Olympian Games in
     Athens, 1896. The First Modern Olympics*
     (Grove Press, 1984), 59.

APPENDIX: THE LEGEND
OF THE MARATHON RUN

1   Plutarch, *Whether Military or
     Intellectual Exploits Have Brought
     Athens More Fame*, 347c; Lucian, *On a
     Slip of the Tongue in Greeting*, 3.

Further reading

On Greek athletics in general

Mark Golden, *Sport and Society in Ancient Greece* (Cambridge University Press, 1998).

Harold Harris, *Greek Athletes and Athletics* (Hutchinson, 1964).

Stephen Miller, *Ancient Greek Athletics* (Yale University Press, 2004).

Michael Poliakoff, *Combat Sports in the Ancient World: Competition, Violence and Culture* (Yale University Press, 1987).

Sofie Remijsen, *The End of Greek Athletics in Late Antiquity* (Cambridge University Press, 2015).

Thomas Scanlon, *Eros and Greek Athletics* (Oxford University Press, 2002).

On the Olympics in particular

Neil Faulkner, *A Visitor's Guide to the Ancient Olympics* (Yale University Press, 2012).

Michael Scott, *Delphi and Olympia: The Spatial Politics of Panhellenism in the Archaic and Classical Periods* (Cambridge University Press, 2010).

Nigel Spivey, *The Ancient Olympics* (2nd ed., Oxford University Press, 2012).

Judith Swaddling, *The Ancient Olympic Games* (3rd ed., British Museum Press, 2015).

David Young, *A Brief History of the Olympic Games* (Blackwell, 2004).

Sourcebook

Stephen Miller, *Arete: Greek Sports from Ancient Sources* (3rd ed., University of California Press, 2004; repr. with an introduction by Paul Christesen, 2012).

Collections of scholarly essays

Paul Christesen and Donald Kyle (eds), *A Companion to Sport and Spectacle in Greek and Roman Antiquity* (Wiley-Blackwell, 2013).

Nigel Crowther, *Athletika: Studies on the Olympic Games and Greek Athletics* (Weidmann, 2004).

Jason König (ed.), *Greek Athletics* (Edinburgh University Press, 2010).

Wendy Raschke (ed.), *The Archaeology of the Olympics* (University of Wisconsin Press, 1988).

Thomas Scanlon (ed.), *Sport in the Greek and Roman Worlds* (2 vols, Oxford University Press, 2014).

On the modern Olympic revival

Michael Llewellyn Smith, *Olympics in Athens 1896: The Invention of the Modern Olympic Games* (Profile, 2004).

Image credits

pp. 4–5 Hercules Milas/Alamy Stock Photo;
pp. 12–13 IURII BURIAK/Shutterstock;
p. 21 Print Collector/Getty Images;
p. 27 Mary Evans/Classicstock/SIPLEY;
pp. 30–1 Robin Waterfield; p. 34 Robin
Waterfield; p. 41 Alamy Stock Photo;
p. 46 akg-images/jh-Lightbox_Ltd/John Hios;
p. 49 The Met/Bequest of Walter C. Baker,
1971, pp. 54–5 Alamy Stock Photo;
pp. 58–9 Alamy Stock Photo; pp. 68–9 Aerial-
motion/Shutterstock; pp. 70–1 Shutterstock;
pp. 78–9 Robin Waterfield; p. 83 Fine Art
Images/Heritage Images/Getty Images;
p. 92 The MET/Rogers Fund, 1941;
p. 95 Leemage/Getty Images; p. 103 Alamy
stock Photo; p. 107 The Met/Rogers Fund,
1907; p. 112 Art Library/Alamy Stock Photo;
p. 117 The Met/Rogers Fund, 1914;
p. 118 Erin Babnik/Alamy Stock Photo;
pp. 124–5 World History Archive/Alamy Stock
Photo; p. 126 akg-images/Erich Lessing;
p. 133 Bridgeman Images; p. 136 By Carole
Raddato, Frankfurt, Germany; p. 139 and
140 Wikimedia Commons; pp. 142–3 © Marie-
Lan Nguyen; p. 146 Bridgeman Images;
pp. 150–1 Interfoto/Alamy Stock Photo;
p. 157 Robin Waterfield; p. 160 akg-images;
pp. 164–5 Science History Images/Alamy Stock
Photo; p. 171 Chris Hellier/Alamy Stock Photo;
pp. 178–9 Robin Waterfield; pp. 182–3 Robin
Waterfield; p. 185 Bridgeman Images; pp.
188–9 Corbis/Getty Images; pp. 192–3 Burton
Holmes/Henry Guttman; p. 196 Bob Thomas/
Popperfoto/Getty Images.

Index

Sybaris 146
Syria 32

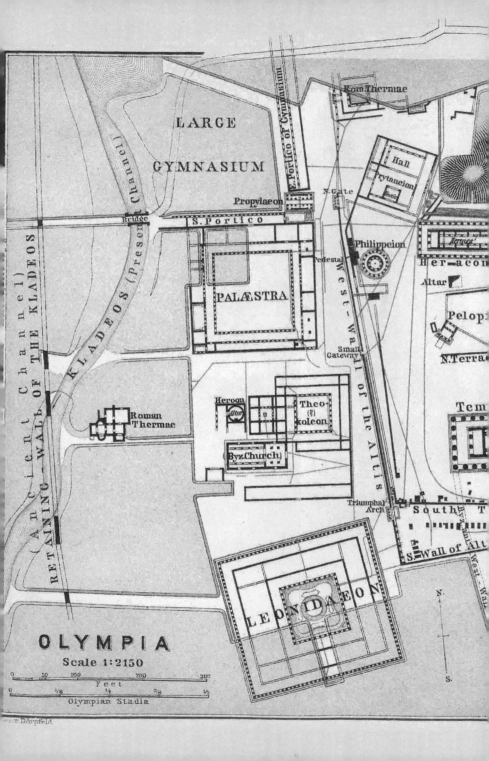

LARGE

GYMNASIUM

Rom Thermae

Hall
Prytaneion

Propylaeon
N.Gate

Bridge
S. Portico

Philippeion
Hermes
Her-aeon

Pedestal

PALAESTRA
Altar

West-Wall of the Altis
Pelopi

Small
Gateway
N.Terrac

Heroon
Altar
Theo-
koleon
Tem

Roman
Thermae

(Byz.Church)

Triumphal
Arch
South T

S. Wall of Alt

N.

LEONIDAEON
West - Wa

OLYMPIA

Scale 1:2150

0   50   100   200   300
Feet
1/8   1/4   3/8   1/2
Olympian Stadia

S.

Dörpfeld.